The Death
of
Learning

The Death
of
Learning

HOW AMERICAN EDUCATION

HAS FAILED OUR STUDENTS

AND WHAT TO DO ABOUT IT

John Agresto

New York • London

First American edition published in 2022 by Encounter Books,
an activity of Encounter for Culture and Education, Inc.,
a nonprofit, tax-exempt corporation.
Encounter Books website address: www.encounterbooks.com

Manufactured in the United States and printed on
acid-free paper. The paper used in this publication meets
the minimum requirements of ANSI/NISO Z39.48–1992
(R 1997) (*Permanence of Paper*).

FIRST AMERICAN EDITION

LIBRARY OF CONGRESS CATALOGING-IN-PUBLICATION DATA IS AVAILABLE

1 2 3 4 5 6 7 8 9 20 22

Dedicated to my wife, Catherine.

For her I have love; for me she has love and patience.

Contents

Preface

In one way or another, the liberal arts and liberal education have been a part of my life for now well over fifty years. Even though trained as a political scientist, I've spent years teaching not only politics but also history, philosophy, law, and sometimes literature. I've also been president of one of the oldest liberal arts colleges in America, as well as chancellor, provost, and academic dean of a comprehensive university with a liberal arts base in the Middle East. Several years earlier I was both the administrative and policy head of the National Endowment for the Humanities in Washington, DC.

Throughout all this I've been writing, arguing, lecturing to anyone who might listen on the declining fortunes of liberal education in America, generally to no avail. Though I see myself as a writer and an educator first and foremost, most people, friends included, think of me as something between a Cassandra and a noodge. OK, as we might say in New York, "It is what it is."

The first impetus to write a book on the nature and significance of the liberal arts in today's America came in the late 1970s, upon the murder of Dr. Charles Frankel. Dr. Frankel was a professor of philosophy at Columbia and the first director of the National Humanities Center in North Carolina. I was a young fellow at the center and I volunteered to help put together the Festschrift in Dr. Frankel's honor, a volume we entitled *The Humanist as Citizen—Essays on the Uses of the Humanities.* This idea of the public significance of the humanities was a subject close to Dr. Frankel's heart. Sadly, too many of the essays turned out to be narrow, semi-scholarly works—nothing that would convince anyone that the humanities had any broader, civic value at all.*

As I read over many of the essays, I saw three conceits at work, each of them with a long pedigree in the liberal arts. First, (contrary to the book's title) that the liberal arts have no "uses"; that they serve no outside, material, or worldly good; that they are proudly and distinctly "irrelevant" to any application or wider purpose. Second, that the notion of the liberal arts as somehow helping to foster something as crass as "citizenship" was a corruption of their high and distinctive place in the world. And third, that true humanistic scholarship is not broad and accessible as much as narrowly focused and academic. I hope, in this book, to show how all three of those ideas are wrong.

The second impetus for this book came a bit later, with the dismantling of the Western Culture curriculum at Stanford. There was at Stanford, before 1988, a core course taken by all freshmen which contained required readings from antiquity, the Renaissance, and the modern era. Criticized as "Eurocentric" as well as sexist and racist, it was first replaced by a more truncated version, then abandoned altogether.

What was amazing to me was not that Stanford would dismantle a perfectly reasonable course under pressure from student activists—after all, I was a graduate student at Cornell in the late sixties, when a whole university capitulated to the self-aggrandizing and anti-intellectual demands of student radicals—but the reasons the faculty gave for abandoning the

---

* John Agresto and Peter Riesenberg, *The Humanist as Citizen—Essays on the Uses of the Humanities* (Chapel Hill, NC: National Humanities Center and the University of North Carolina Press, 1981).

older course. With claims that a "Eurocentric" course in Western Culture was an "affront" to minority students and faculty, that Blacks and other minorities didn't see themselves as "represented" in the readings, and that reading a few great authors in the Western canon diminished minorities' and women's "self-worth," the course was revised to satisfy the demands for ethnic and gender proportional representation.

Nonetheless, what truly made Stanford stand out from the many independent academic minds that were all leaping in this same direction was the double-pronged student chant that echoed round the campus, perhaps even joined in by a presidential candidate who marched with them: "Hey hey, ho ho, Western Civ has got to go!" It was that open revelation of motive, that showing of how curricular change could be simply another scalpel in the service of politics and ideology, which made Stanford the byword for intellectual retreat in the face of the political takeover of the life of the mind.

A few years later another event encouraged me to try to write a proper defense of the liberal arts. It came from a question that William F. Buckley Jr. asked me at the beginning of one of his *Firing Line* television shows. It was a simple question, as the best questions often are: "Do you think everyone should have a liberal education?" Being, by then, a longtime professor as well as a short-time president of a small liberal arts college, I gave it my best shot—a measured, thoughtful, and totally wishy-washy answer. Something like, "Well, while not everyone, clearly, should be *forced* to study the liberal arts, I do think everyone should be given the opportunity to be exposed to great literature, some science and history, maybe some—" "Well, I don't think so at all," Mr. Buckley interrupted, adding something like, "Some people aren't suited for it, don't like it, and we shouldn't waste their time. They prefer to study other things and we should respect that." Nonetheless, I tried again; and, when I still couldn't give a satisfactory response to whether the liberal arts were right for everyone, the conversation moved on to other things.

So here was Mr. Buckley, surely one of the most liberally educated men one might meet, asking a college president to cut through the baloney and talk clearly about the liberal arts. Not sing their praises, not intone pedantically about their high character, not praise them for virtues they may not have, not view them as some kind of universal medicine the admixture of which makes all things finer. No, to speak clearly about them, about their uses and uselessness; about their promise and their limitations; and, above all, about their value to different individuals, value to the country, and value to civilization in general.

The last incentive I needed to write this book came from another question I was asked, this time by three students at the American university I helped found in Iraq. They were freshmen and had just been studying long sections of Thucydides's *History of the Peloponnesian War*. "Doctor John! Doctor John! We have a question and we need to know. Are you an Athenian or a Spartan?" What a lovely question, I thought. So I answered, "Oh, I hope I'm an Athenian—charming, cultured, civic-minded. I wouldn't want to be a Spartan—gruff, taciturn, warlike ..." "No, Doctor John, we don't mean *you*. We mean you *Americans*. Will America stand by us, or will you betray us as the Spartans betrayed their friends and allies? What will America do if we're no longer convenient for you?" It was then that it became clear that history was not, to these new students, an academic study but had real meaning, meaning for both life and death. There were aspects to the liberal arts that had them think, worry, consider, and plan. Under Saddam Hussein, history, politics, literature, and philosophy were meager and always politicized studies, more for indoctrination than for learning. But to some few, some thoughtful and hungry few, after the fall of Saddam a new world was opened, a brave new world. Yes, I know that most Iraqi students were more interested in computer technology or business than in philosophy or history. But every week I had students, both male and female, when I asked what they might want to be in life, tell me, "I want to be a professor" or "be the Iraqi ambassador to the United Nations" or "be a leader of my country." So don't tell me that the humanities or the liberal arts have to be cloistered and useless academic studies.

Once, I believe, liberal education promised to be of immense value to both society and to the individual. Once it promised to make knowledgeable and thoughtful individuals who would, in turn, be intelligent and thoughtful citizens. Once liberal education promised to support the two most important parts of American life—the growth of ourselves as individuals and the betterment of our country. Now, unlike my students in Iraq, it looks like many if not most Americans—students, parents, and teachers—believe it supports neither.

✳ ✳ ✳

Let me return to my conversation with Mr. Buckley. Over time, I've come more and more to appreciate the merit—nay, the necessity—of speaking clearly and truthfully about liberal education. Liberal education and the liberal arts have fallen on hard times of late, and if we think there's reason to resuscitate and revive them, we better not try to rely on the bromides and formulas of the past.

In all, I hope to do two things in this book. In the first part, I will try to lay out the problem with liberal education as I see it today. Some of these problems are permanent and perennial, intrinsic to the nature of the arts themselves. Some are peculiar to the liberal arts in America, devoted as it is to progress, prosperity, and utility. And some are problems we in the academy have foisted on ourselves. In the second half, I hope I can defend and even rebuild the liberal arts in the context of contemporary America. Despite the damage done to our studies by so many who claim to speak in their name, I do believe a restoration and refocusing of the liberal arts for today's society is both possible and necessary.

Contrary to what you might think if you read only the first half of this book, I also believe that, properly understood, the liberal arts are both the depository of civilization and the engine of its advancement. I actually might even think that, contrary to Mr. Buckley, something like a liberal education might be good—dare I say useful?—for all people. But, for the first half of this book, as I speak of the various ways in which higher education has virtually killed liberal education in America, you'll just have to take my word for it.

INTRODUCTION

The Great *Iliad* Question

I was a few minutes early for class. Fr. John Alexander, my high school sophomore homeroom teacher, was standing outside the room, cigarette in his mouth, leaning on the doorpost. "Morning, Father."

His response was to put his arm across the door. "Agresto," he said as I came to an unceremonious stop, "I have a question I've been thinking about and maybe you can help me."

Flattered: "Sure, Father, what's up?"

"Do you think a person in this day and age can be called well educated who's never read the *Iliad*?"

Oh oh, trick question. For sure, I had never read the *Iliad*. I'm not all that sure I had ever even *heard* of it, so what did I know? So I had to fake it. "Hmm. Maybe, Father. I don't see why not. Maybe if he knows other really good stuff..." My hesitant voice was answered by his fully unhesitant voice: "OK, Agresto, that proves it. You're even a bigger damn fool than I thought you were." *

* * *

* An earlier and shorter version of this introduction first appeared as "The Suicide of the Liberal Arts," *Wall Street Journal*, August 7, 2015.

I

I grew up in a fairly poor Brooklyn family that didn't think that much about education. My father went to work right after grade school. He was a day laborer in construction—poured cement, mostly, if the weather was good. Not that he wanted me to follow in his footsteps, not exactly. He thought I should go work on the docks. "Start by running sandwiches for the guys. Join the union. Work your way up. There's good money to be made on the docks. And you'll always have a job." He had nothing against going to school. Except that, if bad times came, working the docks was certainly safer.

I also grew up in a house almost without books. All I remember is an encyclopedia we got from coupons at the grocery store and a set of the *Book of Knowledge* from my cousin Judy. Once in a while I'd head over to the public library and borrow something or other. Actually, I think I took out the same books over and over again—one on tropical fish (I had a tank), a stamp catalogue, and a book by a guy named Levi on pigeons. (Yep, we flew pigeons in my family. But that's a story for another time.) I knew where the volumes were, and I'd always go straight to them. It never dawned on me to look at what else there was. Who read that stuff anyway?

So I guess I'm an educational anomaly—a professor and college president who grew up without many books and without much real childhood reading. No reading, in fact, until eighth grade, two or three years before the great *Iliad* question. Sister Mary Gerald asked me to stay for a minute after class. Did I do any reading, she asked, outside of what we did in class? I told her about the pigeon book and the stamp catalogue. No, had I ever read any *literature*? Whereupon she pulled out something called *Penrod and Sam*, a novel by a guy named Booth Tarkington. She said I should read it. Read it? Why me? I was a good kid. Why was I singled out for this kind of abuse?

So I read the book. Now I can't say that *Penrod and Sam* is great literature. But I do know that reading that book changed a small bit of my neighborhood. Penrod had a club. So my friends and I put together a club. Penrod's club had a flag; we had a flag. (Actually, it was an old handkerchief, now living a second life as a flag.) Initiation rites? We had 'em in spades. Wild war cries from secret spaces? Old Mike, the guy in apartment 6A, who worked nights and slept days, hated us. Penrod would climb trees and spy on the surroundings. We had to be content with climbing on chain-link fences. (It's actually quite hard to spy on people when you're trying to sit atop a chain-link fence.) Our club became, if not the neighborhood menace (as we had hoped), at least the neighborhood nuisance.

Who would have thought it? Here was a whole new way of having adventures, and we learned it from a book. A book, by the way, of things that never happened; a book of stories made up by that guy "Tarkington." In an amazing way, something had pierced the predictable regularity of everyday street life. And that something was a work of someone else's imagination, written down in a book.

So I started to read, and I read with the appetite of a man who finally realized he was hungry. There was a world out there that wasn't just ordinary. There was a world that had in it more than just hard streets, a cramped apartment, and a woman on the top floor who threw water on us when we played stoopball on the front steps.

I became a fairly discerning reader. Well, not really—though I did become a reader of fairly passionate likes and dislikes. Dickens was fine, though he generally could have gotten to the point sooner. O. Henry, Stevenson, then, later, Tolkien, Lewis, Swift...loved them. And even though I thought it a terribly sappy poem, when Emily Dickinson said that there was "no

Frigate like a Book / To take us Lands away," I knew she was telling the truth.

As you may have guessed, I didn't go to work on the docks but wound up studying Latin and literature, French and history, chemistry, physics, biology, and any number of other amazing subjects at the Jesuit prep school Sister Mary Gerald told my father I had to attend. Yes, fathers are nearly all-powerful in Italian American families, but in my 1950s Brooklyn neighborhood, nuns trumped fathers any day.

Nonetheless, as everyone knows, this tension between getting an education—specifically a liberal arts education—and studying something "practical" or simply going off to work was hardly unique to me or my circumstances. Yes (most people might have said back then), this "liberal education" is probably worth something. Reading the *Iliad*, I later discovered, would surpass even my wildest expectations. But so is making, doing, building, and working—so is "knowing other good stuff." And it has been that tension—between the practical and productive on the one hand and the intellectual and more academic or cultural on the other—that I believe has been at the heart of America's historical ambivalence toward liberal education.

✳ ✳ ✳

Keeping that tension in the back of our minds, let's fast-forward to the world of liberal arts education today, half a century after the great *Iliad* question. Parents often still have their qualms about this thing called "liberal education." Parents still ask, "But what exactly does one do with a major in philosophy/ classics/lyric poetry or, further afield, women's studies/queer studies/the literature of oppression and rebellion?" The question might be even more pressing now that such an education runs upward of $50,000 a year, even for some high schools. Besides, with seemingly few job prospects waiting for even the most talented liberal arts grad these days, all students ask themselves the same questions.

Nor is it simply the cost or the supposed uselessness that has buried today's liberal arts. In small ways, the liberal arts have overpromised, or promised wrongly. We have all these lovely phrases, like making our students "well-rounded," that are more or less just words. Are those who study medicine or nursing incapable of being "well-rounded"? Are those who major in film studies or contemporary "lit crit" more intellectually worthy, "rounder," than those who study economics and finance? Having thrown our lot in with that other contemporary shibboleth "critical thinking," we in the liberal arts seem too often to live so uncritically, getting by with satisfying slogans rather than thought.

We overpromised and underperformed in other ways as well. How often have I heard my humanities confreres say that a liberal education makes us finer people—more sensitive, more concerned, more humane? Pretentious platitudes such as these, expressed in today's egalitarian age, are an excellent way to lose one's audience. And that's exactly where the liberal arts are today: In so many ways the noblest and best approach to knowledge and to education that the West has ever devised, the liberal arts are, today, a project without an audience.

* * *

But why do I praise the liberal arts and at the same time scold them? Why do I support the liberal arts while so often chastising the teachers of the liberal arts and the often sanctimonious "marketing" of liberal education?

It's precisely because the liberal arts, when properly conceived and properly taught, are in so many ways the finest education a person can ever hope to have. I do not believe that they, by themselves, make us better people or more humane or (God knows) more "human." I do not believe the liberal arts exist to make us more "liberal," though in the hyperpoliticized atmosphere of higher education you would think that indoctrination into today's liberal political agenda is what the liberal arts are supposed to be doing. No, perhaps they do some things others might find smaller, even ordinary: They show us how look at the world and the works of civilization in serious, significant, and even delightful ways. They hold out the possibility that we will know better the truth about many of the most important things. They are the vehicle that carries the amazing things that mankind has made—and the memory of the horrors that mankind has perpetrated—from one age to the next. They are all that and even more.

Sadly, as I say, I believe that the liberal arts today are often not properly conceived and not fittingly taught. Nor should we make the comfortable mistake of thinking that the liberal arts have been killed by parental philistinism or American materialism and commercialism or the ignorance of today's students or even the cupidity of today's educational institutions, whose excessive costs have made the liberal arts into an unattainable luxury. No, in too many ways the liberal arts have died not by murder but by suicide.

Now, death is generally a permanent thing. But it's possible that a remnant of the past glory of the liberal arts might still live on here and there, perhaps in this fine secondary school or that small college. (If, as we are told, Irish monks could save Western civilization, I'm convinced there's always room for hope.) But I think we all understand that the halcyon days of liberal education are likely over.

Nonetheless, while I will soon rise to the defense of other forms of education, I also know that some revival, even a modest revival, of the liberal arts at both the high school and college levels will benefit almost all students and be a blessing for America as well. What we should *never* do, however, is make the mistake of assuming that some people are a natural fit for liberal learning and others only good for some form of training. Yes, students will go their own ways. But who is "fit" only for the liberal arts or better suited for something else is not a conclusion to be made a priori. Sometimes the children of the Brooklyn poor find their way into the liberal arts more easily than the children of the Hampton leisured. But if the time ever comes when a true liberal arts education can be revived, then I do believe that some of the riches of the liberal arts tradition should be *offered*—in our schools and in our universities—across the board. Some students will then, appropriately, choose other paths. But at least we can then say that the table was set and the invitation sent.

Still, even a partial resurrection of liberal education will depend on something quite radical, quite rare: It will depend on our once again understanding what *good* the liberal arts might be. We might even want to swallow our antique and effete vanity and start talking about the value—the *use*—of liberal learning. Demanding that it be "learning for its own sake" will no longer cut it.

Here's the smallest of beginnings: While I wasn't completely wrong when I said that it was fine for people to know "other good stuff," still I know that Fr. Alexander had the better argument. Some literature (even *Penrod and Sam*) might "take us miles away," but some of it, perhaps the greater part of it, takes us back to ourselves. Some of it holds up mirrors labeled "courage" or "friendship" or "smallness of soul," to see if we can see ourselves in there. It tells stories of Cordelia loving her father Lear, even though her father is a fool. It asks if we would rather be lying a-bed on St. Crispin's Day, or there with

Henry, dirty and cold, facing the armed and ferocious French. It has us walk with Virgil through the dismal rings of Hell and ask at which circle Virgil might turn 'round on us, then walk away and leave us. While our books might not make us "more humane," they can surely show us and lead us to think about all the aspects, high and low, of our humanity. They can lead us to examine these things we call imagination and knowing, creativity and desire, love and treachery, giddiness and joy, hope and fear, and facing death alone.

Even in saying all this, marvelous as it is, we have not even scratched the surface. More than what it can do for us as individuals, never lose sight of what the liberal arts have done and can do for society: not only the preservation and refinement of culture, but the teachings about law and justice, the nature of innocence and causes of moral culpability, forms of government and the ordering of societies. Our literary, philosophical, and historical studies may not, as sometimes the sciences can, teach us the final and absolute truth about these matters, but it can at least help us see the great alternatives, the development of thought, and the reasons the best minds have given. None of this is trivial.

So a defense of liberal learning has to begin with an argument, an argument that might even make sense to contemporary adolescents. Or, if not make sense to them intellectually, at least touch the chords of yearning in them—the yearning everyone has, to know more about love and fear, nature and artifact, justice and merit, freedom and equality. And it has to be an education completely removed from modern indoctrination and political correctness, since among its deepest purposes is to free us from what "everyone" believes. It has to be an education that openly and visibly seeks to liberate the minds of our students rather than capture them.

Finally, is it too much to ask that, if we do begin to rebuild the edifice of liberal arts education, we do it without the superciliousness, the smug haughtiness, that characterized our work in the past? Can we refrain from criticizing the motives or the character of those who seek to satisfy their curiosity or support their families by studying the more practical arts or following a trade or profession? Even though I took the road less traveled, the dream of my father was hardly without merit. In fact, I know I would have learned much by working on the docks. While I'm sure the docks would soon have become just another small neighborhood, another narrow world of friends and enemies, I know that Vinnie the Butcher and his brother Angel would have opened my eyes to things I'm still clueless about. Yes, the docks would have taught me some things for sure, even some things true and good. Yes, the pay and job security would have been better than a life in academia and government. And, yes, there on the docks I might even have found an Achilles or Hector or another incomprehensible Agamemnon. But something tells me it was better, at least for me and I think for many of us, to meet them first in the pages of the *Iliad*.

PART 1

Toward an American Liberal Education

{ 1 }

The Liberal Arts and American Higher Education

What in the World Are We Talking About?

A simple question: What are the liberal arts?

Well, perhaps it's not so simple. Like the blind men holding on to different parts of the proverbial elephant, most people—from parents and students to professors and university presidents—have their own views of the matter. But (again like those with the elephant) even partial views often have some truth behind them. Perhaps at the furthest end, if you ask an average undergraduate what the "liberal arts" might be, you risk being told that they are those courses the university forces all freshmen to take before they're allowed to take what actually interests them. No doubt an honest but clearly not a terribly helpful answer.

Others try to be more exact: "We had to take things like history and literature in high school, but no one paid much attention because we thought they were boring. So now they make us study them in college. I guess they hope this time something will stick."

Now, in mentioning fields such as literature and history, perhaps we're getting closer. It certainly is true that the liberal arts cover subjects that are more "academic," subjects that range from history and literature to calculus and philosophy. That is, subjects that are not in themselves clearly vocational or pre-professional. (Or, as an audacious few might be quick to say, the liberal arts are those subjects that are both boring *and* useless.)

Beyond what students might think, parents and the public itself are often puzzled as well. Many wonder why they must spend so much money to support something "political": "Why do our kids have to study these 'liberal' subjects? Why not 'conservative' subjects, too?" These days, with progressive and "woke" activism entrenched in so many campuses, this question is more pressing than ever. But, for now, let's simply say that while a decent and thorough liberal education will surely make us wiser about politics and the great political alternatives, the liberal arts are not in themselves—or, more pointedly, *should not be*—in the service of any political or partisan stance, whether Tory or Whig, liberal, conservative, Marxist, left-wing, or libertarian.

So, if the liberal arts are hard to define, if they come across as "political" rather than as educational, if too many students think of them as boring, and others see them as merely bookish and with no clear practical value—is it any wonder that the liberal arts have fallen on hard times?

Now, aspects of this predicament aren't new. There has been throughout our history a tension in America's approach to education. To many if not most Americans, schooling means training: the learning of a variety of very practical skills, perhaps as the gateway to a profession. Other Americans think that education should involve something "higher" than training, something intellectual, scholarly, cultural. That historical tension—between the practical and productive and the intellectual and academic—resides at the core of America's escalating ambivalence toward, and rejection of, liberal education.

∗ ∗ ∗

Traditionally, liberal education has always seen itself in the camp of the cultural and intellectual, in the realm of thought more than action. If we insist on making a distinction between "education" and "training," then clearly the liberal arts traditionally fall within the camp of studies that are more "academic" than practical, an education rooted in thinking rather than doing. It is true—non-liberal education clearly has more practical effects than liberal education. But it would be liberal arts pomposity squared to say that the more "practical" arts are devoid of serious thought or that they involve thinking of a lower order. If you forget this observation, rest assured that we will come back to it later.

Now many who defend the liberal arts attempt to make a virtue out of what the liberal arts are *not*. True, a liberal arts education is not, in itself, knowledge of a trade or occupation. It is not training for a profession or for any particular career the way one studies accounting to become a CPA or the culinary arts to become a chef. Rather, we find our studies sometimes described as learning simply *for the sake of knowing*—though learning "for its own sake" is hardly a view that wins many converts to the cause of the liberal arts.*

What else should be noted beyond the contrast between a more "academic" and a practical education? Our students are correct in saying that when we discuss the liberal arts we generally have in mind certain subjects such as history and literature. Indeed, an older view of the liberal arts (in a way

---

* It has to be said that learning "for its own sake" would seem to sell the worth and the true usefulness of the liberal arts for us and for society woefully short.

that now sounds huffy and dogmatic) listed seven liberal arts, no more, no less.* While this overview of the liberal arts seems terribly narrow to us these days, one good aspect of it was the understanding that mathematics and science, and not simply what we know as the "humanities," were also part of this fine thing historically known as the Liberal Arts. That is, the liberal arts comprise language, literature, history, politics, and philosophy *as well as* mathematics, the physical and biological sciences, and the study of the universe with all its complexity and wonder.

For now, let's let this serve as a review: We understand that the liberal arts encompass certain academic subjects, though which ones and how many seems still up for grabs. We also recognize that a liberal education is not the whole of education, but one kind among many. Some argue that liberal education is the finest education. But in doing so we must acknowledge that often it is other species of education—vocational, professional, and many of the studies included in what is now called a STEM (science, technology, engineering, and mathematics) curriculum—that many of our fellow Americans, including our students, see as most valuable. And, as we shall discuss, absolutely no good reason exists to dismiss or belittle this view.

But first, let's talk about the word "liberal."

Why Call It *Liberal* Education?

Why do we say *liberal* education or the *liberal* arts? Why not

---

* Three of the seven—grammar, rhetoric, and logic—were referred to as "the Trivium," and the remaining four—geometry, arithmetic, astronomy, and music— were called "the Quadrivium." And, yes, our word "trivial" does come from *trivium*, much to the delight of giddy sophomores.

call it *conservative* education, since it is an education that "conserves" so much of the world's knowledge? Or, better yet, why not just drop all politically freighted terminology?*

The truth is that the word "liberal," properly understood, is essential to understanding what this type of education stands for and involves. "Liberal" has a connection to "liberty," to being free. And, to be sure, there was a time when the subjects and fields included in "liberal arts" were studies pursued by free men, citizens who had the time and leisure to delve into rhetoric and philosophy or to examine the elegance of mathematics. People, in other words, who didn't have to be too concerned about making ends meet. (Notice, again, the distinction separating the liberal arts from the world of work.)† We carry a vestige of this understanding today; when we think of education, most of us are referring to educating the young—those who don't yet work.

Still, over the years, we've changed the emphasis when discussing the liberal arts in two important ways: first, by dropping the idea that only "men" might be liberally educated, and second (and crucially), by moving from saying that the liberal arts comprise those studies that are the *domain* of free men to saying that the liberal arts are those studies *that help make men and women free.*

Now, having said that the function of a liberal education is to increase our freedom, a myriad of new questions burst

---

* Some institutions modify the idea of a "liberal" education by offering what they term a "classical" education or a "traditional" program of studies. Others call themselves "Great Books" colleges. But these designations seem, at best, a subset or variety of a liberal arts education.

† I know, there is something in us that rebels against the notion that some people dabbled in poetry or mulled over world affairs while others had to cobble shoes or work in mines. I guess we could get on our high horse and decide that these beginnings in aristocratic leisure somehow taint the whole enterprise. But where, exactly, would that get us?

onto the scene. For example, if the liberal arts aim to make us free, how do they mean to do so? "Free" in what way? "Free" to do what?

Consider the liberation connected to the liberal arts. In a fundamental—perhaps even *radically* fundamental—way, the liberal arts are often referred to as a body of knowledge and skills that work to free our minds from being tied up with—or "enslaved to"—other people's opinions. Not that the views of others might not be true. Of course they might. Sometimes "common wisdom" is actual wisdom. But the liberal arts hold out the possibility that we see the truth for ourselves and gain real knowledge about—real insight into—serious and important matters. *In other words, the liberal arts hold out the promise of freeing each of us from the captivity of prejudice, of platitudes and superstition, or of whatever it is that "everyone" believes.* In sum, we advance in our knowledge not simply through faith in what we are told, not by memorizing a catechism of dogmas or relying on what our peers or our culture believe, but through personal reason and reflection—in listening to all arguments and then deciding for ourselves.

Yet here we should be cautious. It's not simply the opinions of others that we should try to think through; we must try to open the cage door of our own opinions—those unexamined notions we assume are true, those ideological and political beliefs and those un-thought-through notions we all hold and that often masquerade as truth. We must be open to all those books, stories, subjects, and arguments that stand willing to help us better understand so many marvelous things. We must be open to moving from opinion to knowledge. We must be open to having our minds grow, expand, and, yes, change. Indeed, this opening up of our minds is the foundation of what it means to become educated.

Consider all it means to break the chains of ignorance or superstition and to think for ourselves. These liberating inquiries encourage us to study history and, hopefully, lead us to see what civilization has been able to accomplish, at what cost and toil, and all the mistakes the world has made and what led to making them. To understand better cause and effect. Or, at times more importantly, to see how a single cause, a single action, might often have more than one effect, and not always the most expected one.

Here's where our various "subjects" come into play. Do I want to know for myself something about the material universe? Surely the study of science in all its fields—physics, chemistry, atomic theory—will assist me. Do I long to know more about life and all living things? I should study deeply in biology, botany, genetics, evolution, and perhaps psychology. Do I want to know better how to live and how to deal with others as well as with myself? Philosophy and ethics, politics and history will help shed light. Religious studies might raise the possibility of the Divine and our place in the universe, leading us to question our faith or strengthen it. It might also help us explore what seem to be common beliefs and practices across so many faiths, as well as what stands out as radically unique—and why. Philosophy should lay out what justice or mercy or friendship or hatred is made of, or what we might see as noble, or it could help us begin to understand for ourselves what might be base or disgraceful even in our own lives.

Literature provides examples of what a life well, or badly, lived might look like, and hopefully fosters a greater ability to choose wisely. Do I need to see models of courage, treachery, magnanimity, compassion, cruelty, wise prudence, and true ignorance? Here we have literature, classical studies, and history. In posing all this we have only begun to name the issues and the possibilities.

We need to go further. It's not merely our minds that are liberated from rote thinking; it's our *imaginations* as well. It was that faculty—the ability to see things not only more truly but also differently—that led us in Brooklyn to imagine new ways of play and adventure after reading even so simple a book as *Penrod and Sam*. Knowledge of the *truth* and insight into what actually *is* are crucial to the liberal arts. But so is knowledge, discovery, and insight into what is *possible*. To paraphrase Robert Kennedy, studying literature, history, science, and indeed any of the liberal arts helps us not only ask "why" but also "why not?"

I could go on, but for now I want to touch on something that becomes important later: These studies and subjects, while they help to liberate our minds and imaginations and help us to live our lives at least partly free from ignorance or mere opinion, also have effects *beyond us*. While we begin with the thought that a liberal education properly conceived and pursued is good for each of us, it might be just as true that the liberation of our individual minds is, even more importantly, a good more widely shared—with our neighbors, our country, and beyond.

Now, if it's true that one cause often has multiple effects, it's also true that one idea is the mother of many more ideas. For example, if the liberal arts are truly arts fit for free men and women, then I imagine it follows that our studies should not be on trivial or small matters. That is, our lives not being infinite, we should probably focus on subjects worthy of the time and effort we pour into them. Having been given the gift of thinking for ourselves, it seems strange that we should squander it by merely thinking about matters of little matter. Thus, the liberal arts seem to be *the seeking of knowledge about important matters through reason and reflection.* Not minor matters, not slight matters, but significant issues of human concern. And learning about them not through "training," not through obedience, not through repeating the thoughts and views of others, but through our thinking, our imagining, and our serious reflection.

While we're still on the subject of liberal education as an education for freedom, let me mention one thing to be careful about, one thing that might seem correct but rarely is: A liberal education is *not* the same as an education built on merely free choice or suffused with "electives." Indeed, very often the least liberating education is the one where students get to pick and choose whatever suits their current fancy or confirms what they imagine their interests are, since it ratifies their currently held opinions and encourages them to run in place intellectually.

* * *

We've covered a good bit in this chapter, perhaps too much. And while I believe all of it was important, I hope we can keep in mind at least the following:

- First, the liberal arts aim to raise us up from the world of simple belief, of accepting things on faith or on the basis of authority, in the hope of freeing us to think for ourselves.
- Second, in working to free our minds and imaginations, the liberal arts challenge not only what "everybody" believes but also what we ourselves believe.
- Third, the liberal arts prepare us not to dwell on small matters but to spend time considering the most important issues of human life. At its best, a liberal arts education aims to inquire into matters of nature

(physical and human) and investigate the meaning of justice and injustice, morality and right, liberty, equality, power, and culture. A liberal education attempts this not in order to give us a passing familiarity with these issues but to help us, as best we can be helped, to see *what might and might not be true.*

Everything we've seen so far points to the profound and liberating nature of a true liberal education, an education that frees each of us to understand, consider, and make our own the most important issues of life and society. But we know that such an education is often seen not as liberating but, rather, as highly traditional and terribly old-fashioned—an education that binds us to the past. Surprisingly, all that is true: the liberal arts are not only a force for the liberation of individual minds but also, at the same time, the most serious preservers of the best and most central works of civilization and culture. In this regard notice this one thing with its full and seemingly paradoxical force: *The liberal arts aim at once to be truly radical and truly conservative.* As an education, they aim at teaching every student to think independently, constantly to ask *why*, to search out arguments and reasons rather than rest on received opinion. And yet, a liberal arts education *also* grasps that what came before needs to be known now, that civilization and culture didn't spring up yesterday, and that wisdom today grows out of what generations long dead have learned. It is an education that frees us to think for ourselves while it teaches us to understand—and as we begin to understand, to conserve, to repeat, and to transmit—all the great works, insights, and ideas that came before us.

Given the importance of this type of education—grounded as it should be in reason, serious inquiry, ideas, freedom, imagination, culture, and tradition—why do we so often hear talk these days of the decline and even the collapse of liberal arts education? Our students still study history and literature and mathematics, no? How can it be that liberal education needs defending daily? Well, therein lies a tale that the next chapter will begin to explore.

The Current, and Sad,
State of Affairs

Until recently, I often got pushback when I pointed out the steep decline in the status of liberal arts education in America. "Why all this depressing talk of abandonment and loss? Do we not hear all the time—from grade-school teachers to university chancellors—praise for liberal education? Now, they may not always call it that. They may talk about thinking critically or about multicultural awareness or about the hundred courses that fill their distribution requirements and electives, but aren't they really talking about the liberal arts?"

Candidly, I do not believe they are talking about the same thing at all, though their concepts are, in small ways, echoes or carryovers from the former real thing. I also know that in more than a few places the old *phrase*—"liberal education"— still exists. But a rich and thoroughgoing liberal arts education seems to me as endangered as the Sumatran orangutan.

When I first conceived of writing this book, I took solace in the thought that while the liberal arts may have declined in the estimation of the world at large—especially among parents worried about their children's employment prospects—within the academy, a liberal education still held pride of place. Back then, I wrote in my notes,

The words "a liberal arts education" have such a venerable history, such rich evocations, that universities and their administrators bandy them about every day. Rare, for example, is the undergraduate college that does not refer to itself as a "liberal arts" institution, even when it might be nothing of the sort. Rare is a university that does not contain within it, at its heart, "the College of Arts and Sciences." Rarer still is the faculty of liberal arts that does not think of itself as the crown jewel of the whole educational enterprise. No matter how professional or pre-professional, no matter how vocational or even technical it might be in fact, virtually every institution of higher education in America likes to claim a connection to the old "liberal arts." It's clear that in the realm of education the words "liberal arts" have always been words of high praise.

How long ago did I write those words? I think it is going on thirty years.

In today's academic world the situation is ever so different. Indeed, it's one sign of the precipitous weakening of liberal learning in America that university administrators no longer choose to highlight their institution's devotion to the liberal arts but, rather, emphasize their attachment to and pride in their STEM departments or the salaries students can soon earn by attending their business school or taking their health professions offerings. Where is the school that touts its philosophy department or classics offerings in this manner? So one way to measure the decay of the liberal arts within our institutions of learning is to see what these institutions praise and fail to praise. And these days they rarely praise the liberal arts.

While I believe that a truly fine liberal arts education can transcend our contemporary division of knowledge into majors and minors, I understand that certain "fields"—English or philosophy, for example—are more closely aligned with liberal learning than others. Given that and given that we live in an age in love with "metrics," here are some relevant facts: Today, by far the foremost major chosen by undergraduates is business. In fact, almost 50 percent of all students focus on just five areas, none of them among the traditional liberal arts: business, education, computer science/technology, engineering, and the health professions. Today, more students attain bachelor's degrees in "parks, recreation, leisure, and fitness studies" than in English. In the race for majors, "consumer science" now edges out literature, all foreign languages, classics, and linguistics combined.*

The situation in graduate education is even bleaker. Of the 833,706 master's degrees awarded in 2018–19, over 42 percent were concentrated in two fields: education and business. Master's degrees in English language and literature accounted for less than 1 percent!†

This is a major shift from not all that many years ago. Then, when young men and women went off to college, it was assumed they would study history, philosophy, and English, and perhaps they might delve into the classics, or rhetoric, or modern languages and literature, all peppered with a dose of mathematics and some science. This is clearly and simply no

* See US Department of Education, National Center for Education Statistics, Digest of Education Statistics, table 322.10, "Bachelor's Degrees Conferred by Postsecondary Institutions, by Field of Study: Selected Years, 1970–71 through 2018–19," https://nces.ed.gov/programs/digest/d20/tables/dt20_322.10.asp. Using these tables, you can make a decent calculation of the rise and fall of undergraduate majors over the last few decades; but note that these statistics do not include community colleges, which account for well over one-third of America's higher education students and where the liberal arts are even further submerged in a vast ocean of practical, vocational, technical, and pre-professional training.
† US Department of Education, National Center for Education Statistics, Digest of Education Statistics, table 323.10, "Master's Degrees Conferred by Postsecondary Institutions, by Field of Study: Selected Years, 1970–71 through 2018–19," https://nces.ed.gov/programs/digest/d20/tables/dt20_323.10.asp.

longer true. Often, when students are exposed to these fields, it takes the form of the ever-dreaded "general education" requirements of the first few years, cast off as quickly and as happily as the university's rules and registrar will allow. Perhaps saddest of all, what was once the most visible embodiment of the American collegiate ideal—the small residential liberal arts college—now accounts for a mere *5 percent* of higher learning in the country.*

Despite this decline in liberal teaching and learning, we often hear the claim that American universities and colleges are the best in the world. And in so many ways they are. Our schools of medicine, engineering, and law are second to none. Foreign nations empty themselves of their finest young men and women, sending them off to graduate study in America to specialize in architecture, agronomy, computer science, aeronautics, or some segment of the great practical and applied sciences, always with the hope that they will return filled with the knowledge and know-how to make their homeland better. So it is professional education, technical education, and highly specialized training that stand at the summit of American education in the eyes of the world. Perhaps there are universities that still proclaim the liberal arts to be the pinnacle of their offerings, but that's not what the figures show, not what the world thinks, and not what American or foreign students go to university to study.

Of course, there are any number of reasons, some even good ones, for this flight from liberal education. A few involve forces more or less beyond our control—the current and universal gravitation toward practical and professional training coupled

---

* See Victor E. Ferrall Jr., *Liberal Arts at the Brink* (Cambridge, MA: Harvard University Press, 2011). Of America's 4,352 colleges and universities, these small colleges number just over 200. And now, in the age of the coronavirus and its aftermath, even fewer may survive.

with feeble job prospects for liberal arts graduates ranks high. But some of the decline is due to our own hubris, narrowness, and self-inflicted wounds. If the final obituary for the liberal arts is ever written, it may read: "This beautiful project died not from old age, not only from neglect, and not exactly from murder, but from self-inflicted wounds that look a bit like suicide."

{3}

The Liberal Arts and the Real World of Work

In 1691, it was reported that the Reverend James Blair, founder and first president of the College of William and Mary, was rudely rebuffed by Sir Edward Seymour, commissioner of the royal treasury. Blair had gone to England to see if he could raise funds to start a university. When he said that he needed money to start a college that would train young men for the ministry and thus help save souls in the New World, Seymour bellowed, "Souls? Damn your souls! Grow tobacco!"

No doubt Blair would have been given much the same response had he said his college hoped to improve men's minds as well as save their souls.

* * *

In many ways, the idea of work defines America. Inventing, making, buying, growing, selling—is there anything more "American" than work? Given this national fascination with commerce, growth, and material well-being, how strange it is that liberal education not only ever took root in this country but also, for the longest time and in its own way, flourished.

Before we move forward to life today, let us begin by considering the time in American history I know best—the era of the founding of this nation and the writing of the Constitution. It seems that we Americans have always been of two minds when it comes to the value of liberal education as opposed to the more useful and productive arts. On the one hand, by the time we established ourselves as a nation, we had colleges of learning in almost every state. To be sure, these were generally founded as religious institutions, but each was devoted to improving the life of the mind as well as the salvation of souls. Nor can anyone today look at the lives of Jefferson or Adams or Madison, or indeed so many of the great Founders of this nation, and not be impressed by the sweep and depth of their learning. We today cannot read a page of *The Federalist Papers* without being struck by the breadth of classical and historical knowledge not only of the Founders themselves but also of those who were reading what these men wrote in the pamphlets and newspapers of the day.

On the other hand, we also knew that we were an agricultural and commercial people, a nation of progress and production, and in any contest between the liberal and the productive arts, the liberal arts often came up short. In his first Thanksgiving proclamation, for example, Washington noted the acquiring and diffusion of useful knowledge as a particularly worthy blessing of the Almighty. He did not mention any gifts of liberal learning. In this, Washington echoed the words of the Constitution itself, which singles out the importance of "Science and useful Arts" as particularly entitled to national protection.*

Even Jefferson (no slouch he when it came to being liberally educated), when in the process of establishing the various schools and programs at the University of Virginia, urged that colleges be set up within the university that would offer

---

* US Constitution, article I, section 8, clause 8.

instruction to such artisans as "machinists, metallurgists, distill-
ers, [and] soapmakers." These various useful, mechanical, and
manual trades would, by Jefferson, have their studies graced
with the title "philosophy." To be exact, they would be called
colleges of "technical philosophy." Remember, moreover, that
the American Philosophical Society, which Benjamin Franklin
founded in 1769, was a society established specifically for the
promotion of "useful Knowledge," that is, for the improvement
of the human condition and the promotion of science understood
as the mastery of nature, not simply its comprehension. Thus,
Franklin would write for the society essays on such "philosophical" matters as the cause and cure of smoky chimneys and on
stoves that could consume all their own gasses. Worthy topics
without doubt, but hardly what we today would recognize as
"liberal." *

Move forward from these early years and examples mul-
tiply, all carrying the same theme: We Americans are often of
two minds in our estimation of liberal education. We respect it,
and we think it must be something important, worthy of great
minds, rarefied, highly scholarly, and intellectual. But we also
praise the useful arts and generally reward the inventor and
doer far more than the thinker. Up to a point, we admire the
intellectual, though we do often snicker at his bumbling and
tell jokes about his absentmindedness and even his blindness to
the real world. We rarely make fun of the artisan in the same
way, and we admire what he knows, appreciating that we profit
greatly from his expertise. We tend to respect liberal education
from a distance while always unsure of what good it produces;

---

* See Eugene F. Miller, "On the American Founders' Defense of Liberal Education
in a Republic," *Review of Politics* 46, no. 1 (January 1984): 78–79. See also
Frederick Rudolph, ed., *Essays on Education in the Early Republic* (Cambridge,
MA: Harvard University Press, 1965).

yet we know what good other forms of education produce, and we support them and encourage their thriving.

Not long after the work of the founding generation was complete, Alexis de Tocqueville noted that everything that is particularly American—our religious beliefs, our habits, our commercial nature, everything—seems to conspire "to divert [our] minds from the pursuit of science, literature and the arts...and to fix the mind of the American upon purely practical objects. His passions, his wants, his education, and everything about him seem to unite in drawing the native of the United States earthward." To be certain, literacy is prevalent in American society, and so the life of the mind is opened to virtually all. But we soon learn that "the labors of the mind" can be turned from learning for its own sake toward something more practical and instrumental: that learning can be "a powerful means of acquiring fame, power, or wealth."

In America, Tocqueville noticed, "everyone is in motion, some in quest of power, others of gain. In the midst of this universal tumult, this incessant conflict of jarring interests, this continual striving of men after fortune, where is that calm to be found which is necessary for the deeper combinations of the intellect?" To us, "every machine that spares labor, every instrument that diminishes the cost of production, every discovery that facilitates pleasures or augments them, seems to be the grandest effort of the human intellect." In brief, unlike science and the arts in more aristocratic societies, Americans "will habitually prefer the useful to the beautiful, and they will require that the beautiful should be useful." *

Move ahead to America's re-founding under Abraham Lincoln. Again, another great statesman, but here—unlike Jefferson

* Alexis de Tocqueville, *Democracy in America*, vol. 2 (1835; New York: Vintage Classics, 1990), 37, 39, 42, 45, 48.

or Madison—a man unschooled in the study of the liberal arts. The important word in that last sentence is "unschooled," for Lincoln was by any measure liberally educated in ways that we who teach those arts can, today, only view with astonishment.* Lincoln had, by his own admission, about a year of schooling "all-totaled." To the best of our knowledge, he never read any of the classical philosophers, no *Iliad* or *Odyssey*, no Sophocles or Aeschylus or Euripides, and no classical history. He never, it seems, read a word of Locke or Hobbes. Instead, he read Jefferson and Shakespeare and studied the Bible and Euclid. He studied to sharpen his mind, to perfect his speech, to find insight into his country's most pressing issues, and to discover for himself models of what a man's life should be like. In other words, though unschooled, he knew exactly what the liberal arts could contribute to both a private life and to a nation.

If anything, our current view of academic life appears even more bifurcated than it was in Tocqueville's time or Lincoln's. On some days, it seems, we toss out whole sectors of learning as mere bookishness and pedantry or, worse, the rubbish of dead white males. But sometimes we think (beyond, I believe, real evidence) the opposite: that "exposure" to the liberal arts, especially the humanities, will certainly make us finer people and better citizens of the world; perhaps, as I said in the preface, it will make us more humane, even more human.

We have the same chaotic view of our teachers. Sometimes we proclaim that intellectuals are truncated creatures, people who think that book learning is a substitute for life, people living in the cloud cuckoo land of irrelevant theories and ideas disconnected from the work and workings of the real world. But then we trot out the professor of literature or sociology or

---

* See John Agresto, "Lincoln, Statesmanship, and the Humanities," in appendix A.

philosophy to help us with every problem, real or imagined. How often, sadly, are we disappointed!

In the next chapter, let's begin to look at liberal education's relationship to the useful, the practical, and the world of work. Let us also start by reminding ourselves that the alternatives to a liberal education—perhaps a religious education, or an education in the fine but not liberal arts, or an education often denigrated by our liberal artist confreres as merely "technical" or "vocational"—each have their own particular and worthy excellences. For unless we see the virtues of other forms of education besides a liberal arts education, we'll never quite understand what our own excellence might be nor understand how we, as liberal arts professors, might actually use the liberal arts to contribute—as these others do—to the greater good.

{ 4 }

Do the Liberal Arts Serve Any Useful Function?

I said at the end of the previous chapter that there are two broad reasons why the liberal arts have fallen on hard times of late. The first reason is, of course, the allure of certain contemporary occupations for which our more technical and vocational colleges are able to prepare students. This would include every institution from community colleges, with their myriad of specialized, practical courses, to colleges and universities devoted to everything from accounting to welding. Second, the decline of the liberal arts as the traditional center of higher education has been our fault. We teachers, instructors, and professors of the liberal arts have had a hand in weakening and undermining the nature and true value of a liberal arts education.

The first criticism—the allure of the practical world—we in the liberal arts see as an easy excuse for our decline since it shunts the blame to others. The second is hard, since it puts the bulk of the blame on our own shoulders, where, sadly, much of it belongs.* But let's start by examining the first issue—the

---

* The inventory of books, pamphlets, lectures, and articles bemoaning the crassness of our American culture and the shallowness of vocational schools or technical colleges is too legion here to catalogue. Oppositely, those books critical

all-too-common critique of non-liberal education that sees our problems coming from others more than from ourselves. There will be time enough for critical self-reflection shortly.

To begin with, we hear that there are troublesome forces in the land spreading everywhere seeds of doubt about the liberal arts. For instance, when my liberal arts colleagues aren't blaming our diminished state on America's love of consumerism and materialism or the general philistinism of the culture at large, they sometimes scrape bottom by trying to fault parents. Now, I imagine there's some truth in this, though rare is the student these days who sets his life's course in deference to parental desires. Still, even though the liberal arts have had a long and distinguished tradition in this country, American parents (not to mention American grown-ups in general, an equally practical bunch) have historically been moderately perplexed by the character of these studies: "I know you like majoring in literature, Suzie, but, please, tell me what will you *do* with it?"

This is a long-standing and common refrain—and one that students and their old-line liberal arts professors were once prepared to talk about intelligently, even if the answer didn't always fully assuage adult worries. We once were able to give answers that seemed sufficiently persuasive to pacify enough parents (my father, for example) and persuade enough students so that our studies generally prospered. But, today, we seem to have lost every argument for our worth when compared to more useful and practical majors, and—while they might listen politely—neither parents nor their children really believe us.

---

of what has become of the liberal arts in America today are fewer. But even if few, they seem to be attacked by the intelligentsia in the academy with uncommon ferocity. Think only of E. D. Hirsch, Alan Charles Kors, Donald Kagan, and (perhaps above all) Allan Bloom. While I have my own varied disagreements with these few, I'd rather be in their company than not.

Let's begin by taking up directly this perennial question of the utility, the *usefulness*, of the liberal arts. Unlike many arguments that defend the liberal arts as rightly standing apart from the realm of practicality, I hope to show that the question of "use" is a serious and responsible question, especially in the American context. Americans have neither the time nor the inclination (not to mention the funds) to throw at an "old-fashioned" or "elitist" education without at least some notion of its ability to connect us to the real world. Nor is it enough—even if we cannot promise a future of great wealth for our students—to emphasize the intellectual satisfaction we *personally* get from our studies and to downplay or overlook the tangible benefits *society* may derive from our education. At least, not if the liberal arts have any hope for support.

I believe parents, and indeed the public in general, have two serious concerns about the value of a liberal arts education. First, the *personal* good gained from a liberal education. The intrinsic value of a liberal arts education to the future life of the student is no longer as evident as I believe it once was. This is especially true when getting a liberal education, thanks to the infinite wisdom of university and college administrators, costs as much today as getting an engineering degree but with little of the hope of secure future recompense.

The second concern is less personal and more societal: Except for the many academic ideologues on both the left and the right who passionately believe that the liberal arts, especially the humanities, can be used to bludgeon students to become cause-saturated activists, more traditional instructors in the various fields of the liberal arts are often so frightened of speaking the language of "usefulness" and "relevance" that they come across less as citizens helping to promote the wider good and more as simply cloistered and inward-looking intellectuals. If we have the capacity and the will to be of real use to society as a whole, many of us have hidden this capacity under a bushel. This was not always the case, nor should it be the case. But it is how perhaps the better ones of us are seen and, I'm sorry to say, often how we see ourselves.*

We need to talk about the usefulness of a liberal education in two ways: first, for each student and, second, for society as a whole. Again, I am not unmindful of the fact that talking about "usefulness" gives most old-line professors in the liberal arts the willies. We always appear more comfortable with divorcing ourselves from utility, with seeing our enterprise as something higher than training people in useful ways or helping people gain a living. I understand this and I sympathize, though only up to a point.†

My aim is definitely not to tell you that today's liberal education needs to adopt a rhetoric of usefulness to deceive

---

* I am forever reminded of one of my best professors, the late Werner Dannhauser, who would tell us about the dream—or nightmare—he said he often had. In it, someone from NBC or PBS would call him on the phone and begin "Are you the noted Professor Dannhauser?" "Yes." "And, professor, you've spent your career studying politics and political philosophy?" "Yes, that's true." "And you've been a student of everything from great literature to history to human psychology?" "Yes, yes, that's me!" "Wonderful. Now, can you tell our listening audience, based on all you know, what we have to do to bring peace to the Middle East?" Silence. Followed by, "Errr...I think there's been a serious mistake. I'm afraid you've called the wrong Professor Dannhauser." I think my good professor was selling himself short: While "solving" the problem of Middle East turmoil was not something he or anyone could have done in any length of radio or television time, enlightening us as to the problems involved, teaching us why the issue is so difficult, and educating us about why slogans or sound bites could never "fix it" was something he could have helped us with. This, in brief, points not just to the practical limits of the liberal arts but to their strange usefulness as well. More on this to come.

† When I first began teaching at a very fine small liberal arts college, one of my colleagues gave a talk on the benefits of the liberal arts in which he argued that our studies had no public face but were simply there for "the management of privacy"—studies whose greatest aim was to give meaning and delight to ourselves. I thought this was wrongheaded then and I still do.

the public into thinking we're something we are not. My point is simply that the liberal arts are, when at their best, not only of immense value—let's even say of "use"—for each of us as individuals but also of value, of use, to society, to America, at large. Keep these two important goals—value to individuals and usefulness to others—in mind, for I believe that the liberal arts are and have always understood themselves as being of great worth to each of us personally and to our societies, our neighbors, as well.*

∗ ∗ ∗

Let me refer again to the American Founders. Part of the greatness of our Founders was that they seemed never to look at liberal education as a stand-alone project, with liberal education here and other forms of knowledge over there, unconnected and untouching. Thomas Jefferson—linguist, scientist, philosopher—had no trouble combining his liberal learning with the serious study of everything from agronomy to viniculture.

How is it that the Founders, who did so much good for our country and the world, seem to have struggled so little joining and melding the liberal arts with the serious pursuit of the practical and utilitarian? If Jefferson could think of a fully educated man as combining farming and philosophy, or if he had no trouble moving from classical studies and history to writing the Declaration of Independence, the tract upon which a new nation would be built, why are we, good Americans all, often so rigid in our separation of the theoretical from the practical, the scholarly from the civic? Indeed, why do my fellow academics

---

* For a look at the awkward ferocity that some in the liberal arts exhibit when asked to consider the value of the liberal arts to America and society at large, see my "Humanists in High Dudgeon: The CFR-ALSCW Standoff," *Academic Questions* 26, no. 2 (Summer 2013): 192–98.

think that a student is "well-rounded" if he takes a smattering of this and that—a course in psychology, a bit of the history of colonialism, maybe a year or two of Spanish, and a creative writing class? Rather, isn't the actual model of well-roundedness someone like Jefferson, who could move through all the marvels of the world, knowing a great deal of everything—theoretical, academic, practical, delightful, *and* useful?

Because I want to break down walls that separate one form of learning from another, let me do something my liberal arts friends always find very strange: let me make as best I can a defense of vocational education.

I would like for us to try to see the many places where a liberal education and professional or vocational or technical education overlap, even join. If we look carefully, we might even see that sometimes the subject matter at the heart of other varieties of study is not all that removed from what we ourselves try to do.

I'm reminded of a talk that Booker T. Washington, the great proponent of vocational education, once gave. He said,

> One of our students, in his commencement oration last May, gave a description of how he planted and raised an acre of cabbages. Piled high upon the platform by his side were some of the largest and finest cabbages that I have ever seen. He told how and where he had obtained the seed; he described his method of preparing and enriching the soil, of working the land, and harvesting the crop; and he summed up by giving the cost of the whole operation. In the course of his account of this comparatively simple operation, this student had made use of much that he had learned in composition, grammar, mathematics, chemistry, and agriculture. He had not merely woven into his narrative all these various elements that I

have referred to, but he had given the audience some useful and practical information in regard to a subject which they understood and were interested in. I wish that anyone who does not believe it possible to make a subject like cabbages interesting in a commencement oration could have heard the hearty cheers which greeted the speaker when, at the close of his speech, he held up one of the largest cabbages on the platform for the audience to look at and admire. *As a matter of fact, there is just as much that is interesting, strange, mysterious, and wonderful; just as much to be learned that is edifying, broadening, and refining in a cabbage as there is in a page of Latin.* *

Words such as these might give you some insight into why I have a hard time with how liberal education looks down on other forms of education. Not only are the boundaries between our endeavors porous, but the avenues of intercourse between us are important and many.

Look at it this way: We in the liberal arts seem to have an infatuation with all things "multicultural." But we limit our understanding of that idea mostly to matters of race, class, and gender differences or whatever new political grouping appeals to some of us at the time. Yet here, in our own academic back-yard, are educational cultures different from us, cultures and ways of seeing from whom much could have been and still can be learned! I have no doubt that both the liberal arts and vocational/professional education could have profited greatly by an alliance with one another. They still can, and they should.

Consider: I know people who have graduated from nurs-ing school who know more real science, more psychology,

---

* Booker T. Washington, *My Larger Education* (Garden City, NY: Doubleday, Page & Co., 1911), 141–43; emphasis mine.

more chemistry, and more biology than almost any liberal arts graduate. I know cabinetmakers who know more about design, aesthetics, and material science than most liberal arts graduates. I know businessmen who know much more economics, mathematics, geography, and politics than most students of the liberal arts. I know farmers who know infinitely more biology, botany, meteorology, astronomy, and soil science than almost anyone with a liberal arts degree. Why are we not doing all we can to be in league with them? Jefferson thought that the fabric of knowledge was best woven from many strands—why don't we?

Take this one step further. Vocational and professional education aims at "work," at least initially. But what all might this devotion to work actually entail? How about some truly admirable habits of mind and character, habits we would have hoped the liberal arts might themselves impart. How about persistence in understanding? How about attention to detail? How about seeing the interworking of cause and effect? How about foreseeing unintended consequences or knowing that single causes can spawn multiple results? Or that one result may have multiple causes? How about order and discipline? How about knowing one's capacities and limitations—and also where innovation and one's imagination might lead? How about insight into the character of the world, both natural and human? How about wonder, about marveling at the mystery, the strangeness, the impossible order, that a farmer finds even as he studies that leaf of cabbage?

This last observation, that a farmer might find a universe of wonder and an infinity of questions in his work, means that, at the highest level, the vocational arts at their best can have much the same character as the liberal arts when they are at their best. At their height, both modes of study can be doors into serious inquiry about important things. Again, why the liberal arts are not more in league with the vocational arts and with professional schools is something I find difficult to understand.*

Long ago we concluded that the fine arts could live fruitfully next to the liberal arts. More recently I think we understand that liberal education and religious education are not simple enemies but can well be compatible friends. Why is it that we fear moving closer to our brethren in the various professional, vocational, and even technical fields?

I do not—I pointedly do not—mean that we in the liberal arts should now go over to our schools of law or business or engineering and lecture them on all the stuff we're sure they don't know. We should not lecture them on ethics or social justice or on how to be more "humane." In our arrogant and haughty way, we've been doing that kind of work for years, and it generally turns out badly both for them and for us.

So what can we profitably do together? How about the best and most sympathetic of us working with the best and most sympathetic of them to recreate some of the courses and environment that once existed when, for instance, law schools actually trained professionals and not simply graduated legal technicians; when the philosophy of law and courses in legal history, developed and tailored by professors of the law, were at the center of an attorney's legal studies; when not merely "constitutional law" but study of the history of the founding and the philosophy of the Constitution were serious legal courses. How about letting the interaction be mutual? Invite a professor of business to make presentations to your classes on

---

* See Matthew B. Crawford, *Shop Class as Soul Craft: An Inquiry into the Value of Work* (New York: Penguin, 2009), for a somewhat different but truly excellent approach to this matter of the value of work, both for our minds and for our character.

the morality of private enterprise and trade or a law professor to come talk to your history seminars about the meaning of the rule of law and its development from antiquity to the present. These examples are merely the beginning.

Second, if this sounds like a call for some humility on our part, that's because it is. Remember that Americans are hardly lovers of aristocracy or aristocratic pretentions. If we want the liberal arts to be respected and to survive in this country, we have to defend the liberal arts honestly, but without arrogance. What we possess and profess is wonderful; but it is not made more wonderful by ignoring or, worse, demeaning other ways of learning. We are not justified because, in our view, others are sinners.

✳ ✳ ✳

One final word on humility. It has to be admitted that our often-unwarranted praise of our studies and our seeming condescension toward other forms of education has a long history. While we can still distinguish between liberal education and other types and forms of learning, I do believe the old distinction between the liberal arts and what were until relatively recently actually called "the servile arts" is now gone. I know that "servile" is the direct translation of *artes serviles* (as opposed to *artes liberales*) and has its roots in Aristotle, in Cicero, in Seneca, and in St. Thomas*; but its use in today's context can

---

* "Liberal studies," Seneca wrote, are alone "lofty, brave, and great-souled. All other studies are puny and puerile." *Moral Epistles*, epistle 88. "Every art is called liberal which is ordered to knowing; those which are ordered to some utility to be attained through action are called servile arts." Thomas Aquinas, *Commentary on Aristotle's Metaphysics*, I.3. Though it must be noted that while Aristotle praises the liberal arts and recognizes that they "tend to enjoyment...where nothing accrues of consequence" beyond the activity itself, it is the useful arts, the "servile" arts, that (in Aristotle's most gentle phrase) "bear fruit." Aristotle, *Rhetoric* I.5.

only be seen as an insulting affectation of the priggish. It was in large measure this older view that led me to explore in this book some understanding of an *American* liberal education.

Still, history is a hard thing to escape. While our rhetoric about the liberal arts is milder and less antagonistic than in times past, I know that we still hear it said, especially by those in the humanities, that it is an education in the liberal arts that produces men and women who are critically thoughtful, analytical, perceptive, well-spoken, and (again) "well-rounded." We hear the claim that students of the liberal arts turn out more sensitive, more understanding, even more virtuous. These claims seem grounded in the notion mentioned before that what we teach contributes to making our students "more fully human"—a claim that must grate fiercely in the minds of our more technically, vocationally, and professionally inclined colleagues.

This idea that a broad and liberal education is a recipe for making people "more human" is one of the great platitudes of the liberal arts today. The purpose of a true education, as W. E. B. Du Bois once famously said, "is not to make men carpenters, it is to make carpenters men." * We understand, and can even sympathize with, his meaning insofar as the betterment of our minds has something to do with the betterment of that part of us, our reason, which is distinctly human. But I mention it here in order to note that there is something quite gratuitous and degrading in the notion that carpenters qua carpenters are somehow not fully or truly men. In the educational sphere as well as in the social and political sphere, it would seem most appropriate to stop categorizing "our" people as "fully human" and others as not.

---

* W. E. B. Du Bois, "The Talented Tenth," reprinted in *The Negro Problem* (New York: J. Pott, 1903).

Well, you might say, not "more human" exactly but probably more sensitive, more attuned to and respectful of the needs and outlooks of others, maybe even—shall we dare?—"more moral." After all, in olden times, we read widely in great literature and learned to have an understanding of, even compassion for, a wide range of human types and human failings. Breathes there a man with soul so dead who does not cry with Lear, who doesn't worry about Jim on the raft, or who feels no distress at all over the descent of Madame Bovary? More currently, isn't it the object of "multicultural" learning to make us more aware of and more sensitive to differing ways of life?

But we have to be careful not to take this argument too far. Are we humanists and liberal artists actually more moral than nurses? Or firemen who risk their lives to save people from gruesome death? Or surgeons? Or even everyday laborers, file clerks, accountants, and owners of delicatessens? Some of the most moral people I ever knew were my grandparents, who not only were unschooled in the humanities, they were illiterate.

＊ ＊ ＊

Let us sum up the situation this way: The liberal arts in this country are declining because most Americans don't see the point of them. They don't get why a person should study literature or history or the classics—or, more contemporarily, feminist criticism, whiteness studies, or the literature of postcolonial states—when their son can study engineering or their daughter get a business degree. It's not only that they and their children want to secure a good job and make lots of money—they often also want to make a contribution more generally to the world, to do something useful for themselves, their families, and their neighbors, even their country; and they don't see what "use" the liberal arts (in their more traditional or especially in their newer formulations) are either to themselves or to society.

Given that pervasive but also understandable attitude, if we want the liberal arts to resume their place in the firmament of American higher education, it's incumbent on us to abandon our clichés and explain two things—first, how the liberal arts are actually of value to each of us as individuals and, second, how our books and our studies are of value to the intellectual, practical, cultural, and even the moral life of America.

{ 5 }

Selling the Liberal Arts: Trying to Be All Things to All People

The process of reviving the liberal arts rests on an understanding of three new "Rs" in higher education—rediscovery, reform, and restoration. Each of these three is difficult, and effectuating all three together may be, in many places, nearly impossible. But we have no choice but to try.

The last two chapters concerned the problem of liberal education confronting the world. What follows is the problem of liberal education confronting itself.

Knowing that this problem of use or practicality is a serious issue for the future of liberal education, we—especially college and university administrators—have settled on a formula we think might help turn this around. It goes something like this: The liberal arts might not be directly practical or immediately relevant, but they are, career-wise over the long run, *extraordinarily* useful. While our studies might not help you land your first high-paying job in the commodities markets, we will give you the skills you need ultimately to succeed at anything you want to do. Indeed, a liberal arts education is the best path to any and all possible future careers.

I do believe there was a time when such a sentiment rang

51

truer than it does today. In times past, we never thought twice about the fact that the president of, say, Proctor and Gamble might have a degree in English from a liberal arts college or that the head of a major news corporation had majored in philosophy. Not only didn't we find it strange; it was perfectly natural.

Today we still occasionally see people in some of the most vital and consequential endeavors whose background was squarely in the liberal arts. For example, when America was going through the riots and racial tensions of the sixties and seventies, it was a man who went to a good high school and a liberal arts college, a man whose studies of religion, law, American history, and oratory gave Martin Luther King Jr. the ability to explain what America stood for and help re-dedicate our country to the meaning of our ancient "self-evident truths." *

More contemporarily, consider Anthony Fauci. Dr. Fauci went to Regis High School, a historically fine Jesuit prep school in New York City. After graduating from Regis but before going to Cornell Medical School, he went to the College of the Holy Cross in Massachusetts, where he majored in classics: Latin and ancient Greek.

But all this was many years ago and, as we know, much has changed—in both the world at large and in the contemporary nature of the liberal arts.

Nonetheless, one thing seems not to have changed in the last few decades: the plaintive voices of college administrators trying to convince students to think of a liberal education not as a premier preparation *for life* but as a pretty good avenue to whatever *career* a student might have in mind. But the problem

---

* Dr. King went to Booker T. Washington High School in 1942 and then enrolled at Morehouse College in Atlanta. Though it offers instruction in various disciplines—both liberal and professional—it still proudly calls itself a "comprehensive liberal arts college." Dr. King received his PhD in theology from Boston University in 1955.

is that our efforts to view the liberal arts as a notable variety of "career preparation" always seem either to overpromise or to wrongly promise. I understand why so many think they have to tie the liberal arts to particular careers—or any and all careers—but it's not an argument that plays to the best strength of the liberal arts, and most students see through it.

A few years ago, Victor Ferrall, the former president of Beloit College, in his fine book *Liberal Arts at the Brink*, gives this example of "John," a graduate of a liberal arts college:

> After graduation, John and a friend opened a high-end bicycle shop. Based on this experience, he subsequently took a marketing position with a major outdoor sporting goods manufacturer and, attending school at night, earned an MBA. He soon moved up in the business to financial analyst. He was then recruited by a widely respected investment banking firm, rising to become an assistant vice president. He later ended his career as the senior sales VP for a large broadcasting company. John worked hard, made good money, was able to support a fine family, and loved every position he had. The question—How did studying English literature, philosophy, some French and geology "prepare" him for this career journey? There's no saying it did, even though it might have cost John upwards of $200,000.*

Candidly, our students understand all this. So if we want to "sell" the liberal arts, we will have to rely on a view of "use" and "value" different from something akin to universal career prep.

"But, but!" you say, "don't be so critical. All we are saying is that a liberal education is good preparation for law school or

---

* Victor E. Ferrall Jr., *Liberal Arts at the Brink* (Cambridge, MA: Harvard University Press, 2011), 108–9.

graduate business school or whatever further education you'll need to begin a great career." Well, yes, there's more than a bit of truth in that. Graduates of good liberal arts colleges most certainly *do* hold their own when they go on to the various professional schools. An undergraduate program in "pre-med" would no doubt have given Dr. Fauci the background to succeed at a fine level in medical school. But was there not something more added by his liberal arts education, something *peculiarly* important and estimable?

Let me put it this way: A good liberal education hardly disables anyone from a future career, even from a highly specialized career. But if we insist on seeing or making liberal education *primarily* "preparatory," we have narrowed and made small the true value, the true uses, of a liberal education.

"But, but!" you again say, "what we really mean is that we teach skills, skills that are extremely valuable, skills needed if one is to succeed in the world of business, or engineering, or wherever." Then follows a list of perfectly reasonable habits of mind and character: The liberal arts teach the skills of clear thinking, careful reading, and lucid writing; they teach us to listen sympathetically and help us to argue persuasively; they teach us how to gather evidence and how to weigh that evidence.

Now, all of this is right and instructive. The usefulness of the "skills" we teach needs always to be underscored. But to put all one's chips on the greatness of skills is, I believe, insufficient. It's like the story of the mother who proudly tells her neighbor that her son was studying to become a surgeon, to which the neighbor replies, "That's lovely. I guess he'll really learn how to use a knife." Skills are important, but substance is prior.

I don't mean to be curmudgeonly, but where, for example, is the older glory of the liberal arts that sought to expose you to great literature, insightful ideas, high culture, or some knowledge of the souls of men? Where is the argument that our subjects might give us insight into the most serious questions of life and help us understand the varieties of possible answers and their consequences as well?

There was a time when the core disciplines of the liberal arts—let's single out English, history, classics, and philosophy as examples—would do all they could to open up the world to students. They would offer insights into a wide range of important matters, into matters of culture and mores, into the ways of the material world and the heights and depths of human nature. Through your reading and study, you would watch arguments being developed and challenged; you might see the tragic results of one awful mistake or how good might lead to even greater good. Given a wide-ranging liberal education, you'd see such things not simply in one field or area but in many. And throughout it all you'd be exposed to clear, persuasive, and even beautiful language. So, with these liberating arts, this compendium of knowledge and skills, of course many doors were opened.

This is why a liberal education was once the entry for any number of exciting and important careers. Looking again at Martin Luther King and Anthony Fauci, the liberal arts helped one of them become a truly eminent leader and statesman and the other a physician of international stature. Their education accomplished something more valuable than entry into a career. It had something to do with making them discerning men of public presence, insight, persuasiveness, and judgment—and thus capable of doing great things.

We mistake the true worth of a liberal education when we try to sell it primarily in terms of career prep. Looking at it in that way easily leads us to diminish our own distinctive value.

Perhaps we try to oversell our mission because we've forgotten what our mission might really be or all that it can actually produce beyond just helping us get a good job.

{6}

Specialization

Trying to convince the world that we are useful in career-centric ways (or even for life in general) has been made ever so much harder as our courses have gone from broad and wide-ranging to studies that are, today, significantly narrower. If it was once hard for a graduating college senior to convince a prospective employer that studying Shakespeare and Cicero was useful, how much more difficult is the task when the fringes of graduate school studies are pushed down into the undergraduate curriculum? That is, given what looks like an increased narrowness and professionalization of our disciplines, is what passes for the liberal arts today still conducive to the breadth we once sought or the quality of mind and imagination we once hoped to foster? Has the movement from reading great literature and taking it to heart been at all advanced by moving the study of literature into the study of literary theory and criticism?

As we've touched on a few times, one of the promises of the liberal arts is not only that they would prepare us to think for ourselves, but that they would also open up for our students an access, an entry, into some of the most important matters of human concern. We promised that we would try to answer—or, if not answer, at least gain insight into—some of the most vexing but central and significant issues of human life.

That said, even the finest study of the liberal arts will never supply every answer. But this we did know: It was primarily through our studies that we would be given the opportunity to address life's most important issues with an open mind and a desire to consider and investigate them for ourselves.

Sadly, while this has always been an uphill fight, I think we all sense that getting students to think for themselves clearly and comprehensively is as hard today as ever, if not harder. It's not that our students have no interest in these great objects of human concern but rather that they all too easily find the answers already supplied. In years past perhaps it was religion that supplied these answers, or the myths handed down through forebears and tribe. In a similar way, today's students get more from their peers, the chaos of internet apps, music, and popular culture than from academic instruction.*

Nevertheless, our disciplines used to understand themselves as counterweights to the reigning culture. Or perhaps counterweights at least in this regard: not that the topics the young gravitate toward are wrong—today most songs seem to be about love, desire, possessing, and (yes) honor—but that the answers given by the culture are so often limited, insufficient, and untutored.† Through the study of history we thought to examine the span and sweep of mankind's activities, including the construct of nations, the varied causes of war, and the conditions conducive to peace. Literature departments would give us

---

* In this way, they prove Shelley correct—poets, including and especially the makers of music and of song, are indeed the unacknowledged legislators of the world.

† Akin to the young collegian who declared her surprise that one could learn about the meaning of love from Shakespeare. She thought, for that, one had to search on Google.

not so much facts, as history might, but works of imagination in which important matters of life were presented in interesting, captivating, and memorable form. Philosophy would tackle the rules of logic, the foundations of morals, the problem of justice. We knew that the breakdown of knowledge into "departments" carried a potential narrowness to it, but it was to a large degree a proper narrowness—the world can't always be examined at once; there's nothing wrong with looking at manageable and related parts and working out from there.*

But what do we now have? Do our liberal arts departments still aim at giving our students a wide range of vision, a look at the heights and depths of civilizations, and an entry into the most serious human questions and the range of weighty possible answers? Not just in America but most everywhere the answer seems increasingly to be *no*.

I have spent the better part of the last two decades working with higher education in the Middle East, where I would see firsthand what a system of education totally imbued with the idea of specialization was like. There, the movement toward specialization begins in high school, where the better students are shunted into science and technology, the weaker students made to pursue something in the arts, school teaching, or humanities.

This continues through university, where you begin your specialty in earnest. You soon become an expert in one thing. For a doctor to know much history or a historian to know anything about mathematics is rare. The idea, the ideal, of a

---

* This division into departments, which take on the aspects of fiefdoms, too often has carried with it the awkward problem of who owned what. Do Plato and Aristotle belong in philosophy or political science? Or perhaps in the classics department? Is Shakespeare in English or in the drama department? If we want to learn all we can about friendship, do we know to which department we should turn? But this is too picky, even for a footnote. I guess we should be happy if such matters are taught somewhere, and perhaps the more the better.

liberally educated person, a person conversant across a broad scope of fields and disciplines, a person who sees the interconnectedness of things and the multidimensionality of the world and events, hardly exists in the Middle East.

Perhaps in this my colleagues in the Middle East are simply ahead of the curve, though we give every indication of wanting to catch up. Consider that in America often the first thing we ask our students is what their "major" will be. We encourage focus from the beginning. We remember that breadth has its partisans, so we pretend that we are liberally educating our students when we have a few "general education" courses they have to sit through or give them an array of boutique classes to pick from to fulfill their "distribution requirements." The thought of truly having an integrated and wide-ranging program of liberal studies, of giving our students the opportunity to see the world and see it whole (as Matthew Arnold noted), is, more and more, simply foreign to us. That journalists or commentators might have their craft informed by a wide range of imaginative literature and philosophical psychology, or a president understand much about the sweep of human history, the principles of political economy, and the nature of the scientific endeavor, is today almost unheard of.*

Oddly, despite our misguided attempt to sharpen their interests prematurely and recruit them as majors in our own disciplines, we often find students who push back against this, who actually do look to their education for some semblance of breadth and wholeness. How many students do we meet who proudly tell us that they hope to "double" or even "triple" major,

---

* I don't believe that when Arnold spoke of seeing the world "whole" he was implying that we or our students would or could ever see it "all." Rather, he meant that we might, through our studies, see the universe of learning as interconnected and not compartmentalized, not merely "specialized."

in hopes that we will recognize and applaud their desire for breadth and some small attempt at comprehensiveness. How often do they tell us that they're concentrating in, say, both physics and music—in the generally vain hope that the bridge between them will span the knowledge of so much that lies between? These are often our very best students, students who could see that what they were being offered in our universities was too narrow, too small, too particularized and specialized to satisfy them. Maybe if they double-majored they could see more. (Sadly, as too many of them find out, only rarely does double-majoring expand anything. Often it means closing oneself off from all else that should be learned.)

I could be wrong, but I have never believed that the impetus to narrow the scope of our fields was a conscious, philosophical rethinking of the best possible content of a liberal education. We came to it, in a sense, back-assward. We started with what we thought our graduate and doctoral programs should look like, then we translated that into what we taught and brought to our undergraduate and high school teaching.

The story isn't all that complicated or obscure. The PhD is a research degree. It's also the "union card" for teaching in almost every college in this country. But the matter is not simply, as we sometimes hear, that researchers are poor teachers. We've all run across good researchers who are also fine teachers. But in demanding that all university professors of the liberal arts possess a research degree that gives evidence of having bored down deeply into a small area, the academy has made a mistake. The possession of such a degree is a poor indication of excellent teaching. There is no necessary relationship between the act of scholarly research and the act of teaching. They involve, we should admit, quite different skills.

Especially in America's universities, but also in many liberal arts colleges, "publish or perish" is the rule. Publish what? Not usually another essay covering with care and thoughtfulness "the same old thing." PhDs are built, and promotion and retention often based as well, on exploring new angles, breaking new ground, being on the cutting edge. "Reinventing the wheel" is hardly what gets one ahead in today's universities. Unfortunately, your students don't know about the wheel; for them the wheel has to be reinvented afresh every time. They're *students*; they don't yet know what the same old thing is, so they need to see it.

I want to delve further into the PhD itself. It's not that a master's or doctoral degree shouldn't signify greater or deeper knowledge; of course it should. But higher knowledge isn't necessarily "research" knowledge, at least not in the humanities. "The liberal arts college...has an intellectual task which is not derivative from research scholarship." Where in our modern graduate schools or in the race to publish or perish "has provision been made for serious critical and reflective thought, addressed to pressing questions which range over time and over the disciplines"?*

The narrowness of modern graduate education limits not only *how we teach* but also *what is taught*. Again, excellence in research is not in itself translatable into excellence in teaching.

---

* Thomas K. Simpson, "Liberal Scholarship and the College Teacher," in *Higher Education and Modern Democracy*, ed. Robert Goldwin (Chicago: Rand McNally, 1967), 49–71. The liberal arts professor, Simpson continues, "must be competent in some field of learning, but it does not follow that it is his business to do 'research'...His business is to teach the liberal arts, to work outward from his own discipline, and to address himself to other questions, but at present there exists only one form of education for him, that of our university graduate schools tooled up exclusively to produce scholars prepared to conduct research. In short there are two kinds of scholarship but only one kind of graduate education" (54–55).

I also know that the narrowness of our research has a seriously deleterious effect on our subjects, on our offerings. That is, doctoral programs as currently structured increase the narrowness of academic departments across the board, even down to the secondary level. If what passes for graduate scholarship is whatever is on the "cutting edge," then undergraduate departments will more and more prize novelty, originality, and faddishness over solid, wide-ranging, and "old-fashioned" inquiries. Doctoral programs are the engines by which knowledge in some fields "grows"; and they are why, in literature for example, cultural studies, deconstruction, reader response, gender analysis, prison literature—you name it—take the place of solid, sympathetic, careful reading of great literature.

We teach what we know. We teach as we are trained. And if we are trained to believe that the edge, no matter how "cutting" that edge might be, is actually the core, then we will believe that students are liberally educated when they take a course called Homoerotic Themes in Contemporary Poetry rather than a course on Shakespeare.

Put aside for a second the relationship of doctoral studies to undergraduate teaching. If I may be so bold, I want to consider the nature of the PhD. The natural assumption, or at least the common assumption outside our ivied walls, is that as a person goes up the ladder of degrees—BA to MA to PhD—that person becomes smarter, more learned. But this isn't true. While the PhD might mean that one knows many things about a particular subject, and probably has written a focused dissertation in an area never before written on or thought of value to be written on, this degree does not mean one is better or more broadly educated. It often means the opposite. While the rise of specialization has been the engine of progress in many of the advanced sciences and technology, yet it has become the cause of so much smallness of mind and vision in liberal arts instructors and in our teaching.

Sadly, this is not yet the end. Among the most deleterious aspects of our doctoral-driven, research-grounded approach to teaching is how we sometimes "professionalize" our courses. Why do so many undergraduate courses culminate in a "research" paper rather than in a well-constructed final exam or an extended thoughtful essay? Is it because, as I sometimes hear, we want students to "think like a historian," or see if they can "apply" the latest techniques of social science research, or perhaps understand the latest in front-line critical literary theory? Is it because we would like to start the process of training undergraduates to be professional biologists, political scientists, or anthropologists, replicating our training and propagating ourselves? But our students don't usually need to "think like a historian"; they need to learn about and from history compellingly presented. They want to learn from fine literature and to have their eyes opened.

It's very odd. We look down on the training of professionals in fields outside the liberal arts, but through narrowness, specialization, and professionalization we transform our own courses into ways of explaining and showing off our trade. The narrowness, the specialization, and the professionalization of our teaching seem to me, sadly, all of a piece.

{7}

Multiculturalism: What Do We Do about Western Civ?

Beginning especially in the 1970s and '80s, "diversity" and "multiculturalism" became the slogans of a new and wide-ranging educational movement. It is a movement that seemed at times to want to expand and at times to supplant traditional liberal education. Despite this confusion of aims, nothing I can think of has transformed the nature of virtually all education more than the idea and the demand for diversity—and all the related educational/political movements it has generated. Indeed, so thorough have been the changes wrought by the multiculturalism and diversity movement—first in the nature of the curricula of liberal education and second in the areas of faculty hiring, student aid and admissions, and the administration of student programs—that I honestly do not believe there will be any turning back, at least not anytime soon. Still, an accounting must be made.

Let's look first at the politics of the situation. The left sometimes claims that the study of our Western heritage and courses in traditional liberal education are none too subtle covers for conservative indoctrination. The right often lends credence to that view with the facile assumption that teaching the history of the West, or the literature and philosophies that grew up with it, is part of the ground and buttress for so many of their political goals.

Both sides are wrong.

Those on the academic right—who not that long ago saw so much of the tradition of Western Great Books as full of alien ideas, irreligion, and corrupt morals (plus nihilism, socialism, and even cosmopolitanism!)—now seem to have become partisans of reading Jefferson, Rousseau, Whitman, Mill, Spinoza, Nietzsche, Freud, and sometimes even Marx.

Especially odd is to see those on the academic left—who were once among the strongest defenders of the Great Books as liberating, even as radical and subversive—now abandoning the field and often, in their search for moral, racial, and gender purity, fighting against the very thinkers and thoughts that originally gave their views credibility. So thoroughly have aspects of traditional liberal education been politicized on the left that any defense of the inheritance of the liberal arts tradition often gets you labeled as anything from benighted to racist.

No matter what side you are tempted to take, it is certain that these charges and countercharges over Great Books and the teaching of "Western civilization," the concomitant push for "multiculturalism" and diversity, the related growth of identity politics, and the onslaught of the politicization of learning at every level have massively upturned our former understandings of the liberal arts. Because of that, I beg your patience if I go slowly through some history and the contentions on both sides, beginning with multiculturalism—what it might say for itself, its problems, its progeny, and its consequences.

* * *

Within my lifetime, the first real controversy started in the 1970s and 1980s with the challenge of "multiculturalism" and its partner, the demand for racial, cultural, and gender "diversity," both in the curriculum and in the makeup of the faculty and student body.

A pivotal moment in this march toward multiculturalism and diversity, a moment that not only roiled all of higher education but also spilled over into general public debate, was the replacement of the Western Civilization course at Stanford.

What had largely been until the late 1980s a Great Books course heavy with readings in moral and political philosophy, and somewhat lighter in literature and history, Stanford replaced with a new required course, which jettisoned most of the earlier readings, supplanting them with works by "women, minorities, and non-European cultures."* This change was not so much an *addition* to a common core—for example, new readings in Islamic or Eastern civilizations or required courses in Asian history or African American literature—but rather the changing of a fairly standard course in the history of Western thought into something it was not.

What was it about this traditional "Western Civ" course that necessitated its "diversification"? What was it about the introductory study of the development of Western thought and culture—once one of the most prevalent of courses in every university core—that meant it had to be revised and reformed? The seriousness of this question was underscored—especially in the public's mind—by the chant that accompanied this curricular imperative. It wasn't "Let's read more minority writers!" but "Hey, hey, ho, ho, Western Civ has got to go!"

---

* I know this history rather well since I was the deputy chair of the National Endowment for the Humanities when the NEH gave a grant to Stanford to rethink their basic course. Little did we suspect what was to follow.

It is my view that how the Stanford revisions began and how they ultimately played out were and remain misguided—or worse. Nonetheless, let me take a step back so as not to be misunderstood. Despite what I see as the serious errors done in its name, properly understood, there's a great truth that lies at the base of multiculturalism. When it is at its best, liberal education has always been *particularly* multicultural—and it is truncated and diminished if it is not. As a world-class liberal arts professor of mine (masquerading as a mere graduate school political scientist) once told as many of us who would listen, there are two things all educated people must know: First, they must first know their own. Second, they must also know what is *not* their own.

They must know their inheritance—their literature, their common history, the principles their country is founded upon and the difficulties inherent in living up to those principles, the lives of their most important as well as their most ignoble men and women, the highlights of their culture's art and music, their central religious traditions, and something of the principles of science that have shaped their modern world. But they will never really know their own unless they also know the great *alternatives* to their way of life. If all our students see is their own—and of that, now, ever so little—they are simply uneducated.*

A strong case could be made that the books on Stanford's original course list gave all students a serious academic introduction to the development of thought within the Western tradition. In other words, it did a more than decent job offering students insight into what was "their own." But the importance of the history of Western thought is not simply that it enlightens us

---

* For one take on this, see "Why Latin, Why Greek?" in appendix B. As a follow-up to this view, see also Cornel West and Jeremy Tate, "Howard University's Removal of Classics Is a Spiritual Catastrophe," *Washington Post*, April 19, 2021.

to what is "our own" but that it also makes clear the historic alternatives and the great turning points in our development. Indeed, the various ideas that animate today's reformers—ideas and ideals of equality, freedom, individualism, self-actualization, feminism, relativism, anti-racism, anti-clericalism, historicism, and more—have all been started, nurtured, fought over, and defended or rejected primarily here, in the authors, philosophers, and Great Books of the West. There is no "liberal education" without those books.

The issues taken with the various Great Books courses and so many other aspects of traditional liberal education seldom seem to rest on any supposed weakness other than their *political* weakness. That the books Stanford students were once assigned to read might well be intellectually stimulating, or that almost all of them might have been pivotal in shaping the direction of Western life, is now deemed beside the point. Even the argument that, taken together, these books are hardly consistent—that they contain perhaps the greatest, most serious, and most radically "diverse" views that our culture has entertained (e.g., Plato versus Marx, the Hebrew Bible versus Freud or Darwin, Dante and Pascal versus nearly every aspect of contemporary culture)—does not matter. What matters is that many of these viewpoints seem to conflict with the political views of today's political/educational reformers. To these reformers, the disagreements among the thinkers of the past might make such thinkers seem a curiosity. But their potential disagreements with the worldview of present-day activists make them not worthy of study but, rather, the enemy.

What was lost with the "going" of Western Civ was the opportunity for Stanford students and then many others to start on the path to being liberally educated and to see the growth and grand sweep of the finest literature and most pivotal thinking and arguments that shaped our culture and, most importantly, shaped their own lives.

$$* \quad * \quad *$$

From the beginning the multicultural/diversity movement had all the right words, words like "openness" and "inclusivity." But with the call for diversifying the curriculum it soon became apparent that something had changed. It was originally argued that all that was studied before would be enriched, opened up, and made more inclusive. But it never seemed to work that way. Indeed, the saddest thing about the great multicultural movement was not that it fell short of revivifying the core with the important works and deeds of others but that it ultimately resulted in the non-integration of other cultures into a common core.

Soon it was understood that the fight for multiculturalism in curricular matters could not end there. It carried with it the empowerment of, and thus the politics of, special interest groups. Rather than treating all students as students, as opposed to gay students or Chicano students or women students, the push for greater "diversity" meant that each discrete group had a stake in "their" books and in "their" studies being protected and advanced. We saw the movement toward diversity—which began as a call for inclusion—quickly devolve into the separation and then politicization of distinct interests and worldviews. And what began as a movement toward openness and inclusion has, instead, heightened the divides and made rigid the separations.

If the basic view of diversity as inclusion and greater conversation among and between cultures had a rational basis in educational theory, this growing understanding of diversity as separation was hardly broadening, hardly liberal, and thoroughly political.

For all the talk of getting students to think cross-culturally, encouraging students to break out of their limited cultural horizons and see the world in all its larger complexity, one result of the new and growing "diversity" movement was to build monocultural programs and encourage some of the best students to focus their efforts in that field, the area of their "identity." Thus, concentrating in the Great Books of the West is a Eurocentric sin, majoring in Chicano studies a great virtue. Forgive me, but those looking at this are to be pardoned if, rather than solid educational reform, we see a rejection of the common culture as well as an ideological (as opposed to an educational) program at work. In narrowing the focus of their learning to the demands of contemporary ideology or the politics of special interests, they have made the broad sweep of the history of Western knowledge small and dismissible—three millennia of learning and imagination in art, literature, music, poetry, philosophy, all jettisoned.

What began with the rhetoric of expansion soon became the politics of smallness.*

* * *

What might a serious multicultural education look like or contain? It could attempt to gain new insights into humanity's perennial questions by looking more deeply at other civilizations and cultures. This might mean, for example, expanded studies of Latin American history or the character of Japanese art or teaching Chinese more thoroughly. The multicultural

---

* "The sad result of the humanities' use of racial and gender diversity as a criterion for the selection of texts and teaching methods has therefore been to make it harder to pursue the question of life's meaning in the only disciplines in which there is any chance of asking it." Anthony T. Kronman, *Education's End: Why Our Colleges and Universities Have Given Up on the Meaning of Life* (New Haven, CT: Yale University Press, 2008), 153.

movement never seemed to suggest the study of Farsi or Arabic or that we pay close attention to the words of the Koran, the history of Islam, or the sayings of Mohammad, with all the significance that would have had for our contemporary and future national life. There was no real attempt to look at another high culture or civilization and use that either to supplement our understanding of things European and American or even to contrast the knowledge and insights of that culture with our own.

Perhaps part of the reason why a true multiculturalism failed to take hold in higher education was because, properly pursued, it could easily teach a myriad of inconvenient truths. A true liberal education is not just reading the best that has been thought, said, and done but also coming to grips with the very worst that has been said and done and understanding why. In that regard, a *true* multiculturalism could still do at least some of what the new dispensation is looking for, namely, to help us see the contrasts or contradictions in our own culture more clearly. But it can also do much more: A true multiculturalism—comparative history, comparative cultural accomplishments, comparative literature, religion, and philosophy—might help us understand better not only our shortcomings but, by comparison, our achievements as well. A true education in diversity might help us see evil comparatively. We might understand American slavery in the light of Islamic slavery, African slavery, and slavery and oppression under various other ideologies.

But that would only be the beginning. Two other insights might result from this: first, a better understanding of what might be the religious, ideological, and economic bases of much of human oppression and, second, the degree to which religion, philosophy, and economics have had a role in mitigating or reversing much of human cruelty.

Furthermore, on an even deeper level, an honest multiculturalism might give our students the opportunity to ask a truly serious question. Is oppression cultural—that is, as so many seem to believe, formed by society and social structures and "systemic" to that culture—or something intrinsic to the character of humanity itself? And if it is intrinsic and natural, then what arguments, what experiences, what moral teachings, whether from the West or the East, have been seemingly so powerful that they have been able *to modify our natures* such that racial and sexual oppression are increasingly (though hardly universally) seen as unjust and slavery is now almost everywhere understood as evil? This would unquestionably be an education useful to our own future and the futures of other nations.

Thus, we could finally ask what was it that caused the notion of human liberation to flower—what ideas, writings, religious principles, or events brought about these current views of human equality, individuality, and freedom that so many contemporary believers in liberty, liberation, and equality cavalierly take as true. This would be the wonderful fruit of a real liberal education—one that seeks insight in books, reason, and arguments rather than weakly standing on slogans. No serious matter of life, society, or human relations hasn't been studied and fought over in our history or in the pages of our greatest books.

But the diversity/multiculturalism movement seemed never to have an interest in these kinds of serious questions. The movement appeared to have two main aims, aims that were surely contemporary but which never rose to the heights of what a true multicultural education might teach. First, it was an attempt to ratify the history and literature of groups that currently felt slighted or victimized by the European or American experience, primarily Blacks, women, Latinos, and homosexuals. Second, and more importantly, it was an attempt to weaken the central role of the West, its history and its ideas, and deny its having substantial merit or intrinsic worth. "Hey, hey, ho, ho, Western Civ has got to go" were words that meant something to those who marched for the new Stanford curriculum, something, sadly, quite extraordinary in higher education.*

---

* For a more detailed account of what Stanford did and for further reflections on diversity, see appendix C.

{8}

Politicization: From Freeing Minds to Capturing Them

The growth of identity politics on college campuses is only one part of the larger issue of the politicization of higher education and the decline of liberal education today. Connected to it is the movement to penalize and purge from the university any positions, books, thoughts, and arguments that run contrary to student sensitivities or current social and political orthodoxies. Debates over what *should* or even *must* be taught to mold and direct students has a flip side—what *cannot* be taught, what *may not* be spoken. Speech codes, "trigger warnings," safe spaces, proscribed pronouns, the banning of speakers, the privileging of some types of speech and ideas, and the forbidding of contrary utterances—all this is of a piece with the desire to indoctrinate and to do it in the name of teaching.

These anti-educational movements seem to be virtually everywhere on American college campuses. Yet, in some ways, we shouldn't be surprised. The desire to use education for political purposes, to treat universities as seminaries for the promotion of our views or to entice students to become activists for our cause is hardly new. As Julien Benda wrote of the politicized academics of his day who lent themselves to the cause of Fascism, romantic nationalism, and class justice on the right, they have "the thirst [for action and] for immediate results, the exclusive preoccupation with the desired end, the scorn for argument, the excess, the hatred, the fixed ideas." *

Coming closer to this century, we have the president of Yale warning, "The greatest threat to academic freedom today is not from outside the academy, but from within. Political correctness and 'speech codes' that stifle debate are common on America's campuses. The assumption seems to be that the purpose of education is to induce correct opinion rather than to search for wisdom and to liberate the mind." †

Still, rather than begin with a list of all the disasters visited of late on our universities that are included under the phrase "politicization" or "political indoctrination," let's consider how the side accused of politicizing collegiate teaching understands itself. After all, the liberal arts are at their best when they encourage us to view things not simply critically but also sympathetically, especially when confronted with ideas and positions with which we think we disagree. If, under the guise of serious teaching, there are those who try to propagate their social and political views and to silence those who differ, we owe it to ourselves to ask why.

Perhaps this is kindest way to view it: We have all sat through tedious lectures given by monotonous professors who could

---

* Julien Benda, *The Treason of the Intellectuals* (1927), trans. Richard Aldington (New York: Norton, 1969), 46. The obsessions of his day, writes Benda, were "racial passions, class passions and national passions" (3). Today, the triplet is race, class, and gender. Notice how easily this enthusiasm morphs from left to right, from liberal to fascist, simply by substituting "nation" for "gender." Or, to look at it slightly differently, I do not think the left sufficiently understands that "culture" is a *deeply* right-wing concept.
† Benno Schmidt, "Universities Must Defend Free Speech," May 6, 1991, reprinted in the *Wall Street Journal*, December 8, 2015, https://www.wsj.com/articles/notable-quotable-benno-schmidt-on-free-speech-1449532954.

make even the most fascinating subject lifeless. How refreshing it is to have teachers so excited by their subjects that no matter what they might profess—French grammar, petroleum engineering, the philosophy of Plato—their passion is infectious. As long as they're not silly or daft in their enthusiasm, it is those teachers, not the drones, that all students remember.

We can admit from the start that there's a bit of the fire of St. Paul in all great teachers: an attachment to what they know and a desire to make their students, at least in part, love what they love and accept the truth as they themselves view it.

But this passion cuts two ways. It's a fine line between educating our students so they soon have the wherewithal to possess their own minds and trying to possess our students' minds ourselves. Moreover, the passion to capture minds rather than to free them—to have our students see the world our way and side with us—is always felt more strongly the greater the stakes seem. To be passionate about Latin verbs is one thing, harmless and even charming. But to be passionate about things sectarian or political, about movements and activism, about what we should so love or hate that we would march to the barricades for it or silence others, is neither harmless nor charming.

For a teacher to have the passion of St. Paul is one thing; to have the aims of Paul to instruct in order to convert or capture is something else. And the higher the stakes—acceptance of the true faith, views on social justice, the belief that we should destroy American hegemony, a desire to further ethnic or racial solidarity or to advance the status of women or to celebrate and promote or despise and condemn alternative lifestyles—the greater *always* is the impetus to indoctrinate rather than to educate and free.

To put it another way, one reason it's difficult to get politics out of the classroom is that it's hard to get politics out of people. We all have our ideas of right and wrong, of what's just and unjust, and it is hard not to want others to believe and act as we do. This means that the desire to indoctrinate, to make our students see things our way, is never far from the act of teaching. But that hardly excuses it. In the end, indoctrination is the dark and evil twin of teaching. Why is this problem of politicization so prevalent in the liberal arts rather than, for example, in engineering or schools of agriculture? And why, in the liberal arts, is this problem most apparent in the humanities?

While every great physicist loves his field, no professor has a moral stake in whether a particular student believes in the second law of thermodynamics or not. You either understand it or you do not; there's no "believing" in it or not; and the world doesn't change—or even much care—if you reject it. Besides, you can demonstrate all you want in opposition to it, but rest assured—nothing will change.

In contrast, the humanities have, at their heart, always tried to understand important political and social ideas such as justice and merit, freedom and community, good and evil, and much may well hinge on whether the next generation embraces a teacher's particular views. A student's belief in this regard might even mean as much to some professors as an affirmation of religious orthodoxy meant to the Spanish Inquisitors. And often, one might argue, with similar results.

So it's understandable that the impetus to politicize might so peculiarly find a home in humane studies, given an instructor's passion for teaching coupled with an intrinsic connection, in the humanities, to what today are lightly called "values."

But, still, how bizarre, how utterly perverse it would be to find at the very core of the liberal arts, the "liberating" arts, not an attachment to freeing students to examine all sides and then think for themselves but a serious and regular attempt to encourage, shame, bully, and sometimes compel attachment to a set of prescribed values and beliefs.*

In the late sixties and early seventies, as a graduate student at Cornell, I was witness to the destructive campaigns of the Students for a Democratic Society (SDS) and the black power and anti-war movements that shut down the university and forced the administration to accede to their demands. To these students at Cornell and to those like them elsewhere, it was clear that the battle to upend American higher education would be fought in the soft underbelly, so to speak, of the university: the humanities.

But looking back on those events, some things about their demands might seem inconsistent with their stated goals. Inconsistent since one might have thought that radicalizing the business schools because of their corporate ties and often bourgeois values or attacking departments of science for the support they indirectly gave to modern technology and the fundamental character of modern life would have ranked higher on the list than the departments of history or literature. There was some movement in the law schools to make them more in tune with revolutionary thinking. Nonetheless, it soon became clear that it was in the humanities where the substantive revolution would take place.

---

* There's a strange notion that seems to live at the heart of the argument against, for example, the reading of Great Books, that the professor who promotes the reading of these books does so in order to compel or "convert" the student in some way—for instance, that we have our students read the Bible to make them Christian or "religious," that we have them read Locke and Smith to make them liberal capitalists or Marx to make them Marxists. This can only be believed by those who must treat books that way in their own classes; that is, they prescribe books to compel the student's belief or to assent to what the book says. Is it so far beyond comprehension that one might ask students to read something so that they might take seriously the arguments and understand what is being said?

Yet the reasons for this are hardly hidden: The humanities have always been central to this project called Western civilization. There, in the liberal arts as a whole and the humanities in particular, is where the culture in all its aspects resided.

In saying that the spirit of this culture had its home in the liberal arts, I don't mean anything pretentious or mystical. What we know as Western civilization comes to us primarily through its history, both secular and religious; through the works of its cultural and political actors; and through its thinkers, artists, and authors. Western civilization explains itself and lives on through its works—its books, documents, monuments, churches, biographies, buildings, art, and music. If one wishes to make not simply an immediate change but a more permanent change, a world-historical change, a change in human history, one should go to the heart. The world has been told repeatedly that the humanities were "the repository of civilization." Then where else should revisionists go who would change our minds and reform "civilization"?

Sadly, in far too many places, today's liberal education seems to aim less at freeing the imagination of our students than in capturing their thoughts, less at liberating their minds than at controlling their minds. And for those students who are already true believers, the classroom is now a place that will both underline their beliefs and openly push their activism. What was before seen as a liberating education now comes across as social and political indoctrination, an indoctrination-cum-activism overlaid with all the moralism, piety, and self-righteousness once associated with dogmatic and narrow sectarianism. Is it any wonder that university administrators understand that the safer public stance is to promote their institutions' offerings in science, technology, engineering, and mathematics than in the humanities?

Abandoned by large swathes of the public and by many universities, the liberal arts find themselves eviscerated, a shell of their former selves. Looking over the landscape of higher education today, academic ideologues might think that the ideological battles were won by themselves and their partisans. But the wider war was lost. The liberal arts—once the ground and starting point of all higher education—have been marginalized. The broader culture, which had its doubts about the value of the liberal arts even in the best of times, has now simply walked away and left the corpse to the victors.

{9}

The Denigration of the High

In its promotion of fine literature and serious thinkers, liberal education has always pushed against the inclinations of democratic sensitivities. As we have noted, calling something "high" or "great" often conflicts with old-fashioned American egalitarianism. But the current denigration of the high, as I've labeled it here, seems different. It has far more *ideological* roots than anti-elitism, populism, or any pro-egalitarian sentiment.

Every day we read about the toppling of those towering figures that once stood as the educators of our civilization. Aristotle? "Why, he was a sexist, wasn't he?" Homer? "I was told he glorifies war and killing." Jefferson? Washington? "Weren't they racists, along with maybe Lincoln, too?" Dante? "I heard he's intolerant, religious, and judgmental." The Bible? "Patriarchal and homophobic." America? "That's that hypocritical country where people owned slaves, that keeps down the poor, and that kills and starves people overseas while it destroys the world's environment. I know all about it; I learned it in high school."

The centrality of those writers and thinkers that liberal education has always focused on is today seriously diminished. But they are not being pushed aside because they are elitist figures who think they're better than us. Nor did the study of

Western Civ at Stanford "have to go" because it was demanding or haughty. No, it was the *moral* failings, the politically incorrect character of earlier writings and thoughts, that make these figures the enemies of today's ferociously held political religion.

Liberal education lives in the constant hope of discovering the truth about the most important things. But if the truth is now more fully grasped, if the meaning of justice is now clearer than ever before—and if views contrary to current academic beliefs and sensibilities are sexist, racist, homophobic, or even simply upsetting—then justice demands the books and works of traditional liberal education be put aside or, at worst, attacked and "canceled."

For a while there may have been hope that something like the old Great Books courses, courses that still have a foothold at Columbia, Chicago, St. John's, and elsewhere, might prop up humane education. But this is more often than not a slender hope. With the Great Books (now usually referred to by their detractors as "the so-called great books") harboring so many tainted rogues in its gallery of dead white males, there seems little appetite to go there for much collegiate enlightenment these days.

Before, I noted that the highest argument for a liberal education was that it gave us an awareness of what is ours and serious insight into what is not ours. This applies with even heightened force today. I can think of nothing more destructive of education itself than to erase, to "cancel," the thoughts and writings of those who have contributed to making us who we are—or who clearly show us who we are not—simply because they don't share our current prejudices or abide by all our latest opinions. Because so many serious thinkers and books are now seen as "other," they are perhaps even more essential than ever for us to know. If these thinkers have insights that we've become blind to, or thoughts that are far from our own, or arguments that we have failed to confront—and all these on matters important for life—then to demean them and cast them aside without study is more than foolish; it is the polar opposite of becoming educated.

This is not just an argument for taking seriously the peaks of human thinking, literature, and art; but also many important works below them. In my own field, we understand better the Founders' Constitution by reading the writings of the various Anti-Federalists alongside *The Federalist Papers*. We understand our type of democracy better if we study the skeptics and early critics of our way of life. The debate between Edmund Burke's conservatism—grounded as it is in history and national culture—and Thomas Paine's America, based on pluralism and universal rights grounded in nature, is as necessary to grasp today as it was in the eighteenth century. To comprehend the causes of the Civil War not only do we need to study Lincoln, but we need to look at the positions of people such as Stephen Douglas and Frederick Douglass, Harriet Beecher Stowe and the abolitionists. Indeed, to understand fully both the real radicalism of Jefferson's egalitarianism and the unprecedented nature of Madison's Constitution, there's no more comprehensive attack on these views than the writings of the much-reviled John C. Calhoun.

I understand the rejoinder that liberal education in America is and has always been under attack. Often the popular American right pushes every kind of education but liberal education; McCarthyism and the anti-Communist campaigns of the fifties were imbued with a fierce "cancel culture" of their own. There are even some dogmatic conservative and sectarian colleges that may think of themselves as defenders of liberal education but are as doctrinaire as the most left-leaning colleges. Many times did I, as president of St. John's College, need to defend our assigning Marx as part of our Great Books offerings. I'm sorry, but without understanding Marxism by reading Marx himself, we ourselves will have no clear understanding of the recent past trajectory of Western civilization, or of the consequential and real debate about the power of ideas versus the power of economic determinism, or of the many issues of economics and equity we still and will face as a nation.

So, yes, you might think the liberal arts have weathered so many storms that they will weather this. But notice: Almost all the political attacks I've mentioned came from without. They came from ideologically driven public sentiment and from powerful politicians. They were promoted as part of the agenda of clearly sectarian political/religious institutions. These opponents of liberal higher education we could and did withstand. But today the dismantling of the liberal arts comes from the professors, students, and administrators within bedrock universities and liberal arts colleges. It comes from radicalized departments of history, literature, classics, American studies, and all the myriad of other studies connected to ethnopolitical interest groups. It comes from virtually every school and college of education.* This is why I have no hesitation in saying that liberal education in America is dying not by murder but by suicide.

* * *

Just as significant thinkers, great books, standard histories, and fine literature were being trashed in many schools and universi-

---

* It may be true, for example, that critical race theory, as such, is not being taught in our classrooms. But pick up virtually any College of Education catalogue of any major university and take in the full compendium of courses on race, privilege, whiteness, and grievance activism being taught as part of the curriculum of our *teachers*.

ties, the vacuum was partly being filled with online Great Books programs, internet Socratic discussion programs, TED talks, serious private book clubs, and the like. None of these are a substitute for a sustained collegiate liberal arts education, but they are an indication of the loss felt by Americans across the board. I hope the arguments and ideas in this book will give them solace and courage.

But let me return to the issue of substituting social/political indoctrination for traditional education and erasing any serious education that was founded on nearly 3,000 years of learning.

I know that most of my compatriots who work hard to defend traditional liberal education spend many waking hours decrying the thousands of attacks on free speech and academic freedom. And, yes, the shouting down of speakers or disinviting them, the burning of conservative student newspapers, and the silencing of alternative viewpoints are serious and seriously indefensible. But I feel the need to look deeper. The problem goes further than free speech and disinvited lecturers, further even than professors peddling their politics in class and badgering students. It concerns the toppling and ruin of traditional education itself.

To see firsthand the overthrow of traditional education and how the teaching of the liberal arts has become fully politicized, go right to the source: the academic course catalogue. The interesting thing about college and university catalogues is that they tend to be forthright about what they are doing. As Mr. Berra might say, you can learn a lot just by reading.

What would perusing a range of these catalogues, say from the early sixties to the present, reveal? First, you'd notice that in many if not most places there was a "core"—a required set of basic courses that introduced the new student both to a range of academic disciplines and to some subjects thought to be central to becoming an educated person. Here were language requirements, a literature survey course, usually an intro to Western civilization, and a math and a general science course required of everyone. These were not what we know of today as "distribution requirements" but, rather, a set of courses that were to be taken by all students covering the first year of study and often going into the second year.

Under the new understanding, these core courses were among the first to be abandoned as requirements (Stanford dropped its new Civ core, for example, after eight years, in 1997). Here and there, distribution requirements took their place, but in many schools students were now free to take any course they found interesting, so long as basic preceded more advanced.

But we should not jump to the conclusion that the idea of a required core set of courses was everywhere gone. In a strange twist, in place of the old "dead white male" courses, courses that preached diversity and inculcated sensitivity to minority, feminist, and gay/transgender concerns would often serve as new "core requirements" that all students were obliged to take. Over time, this new and highly ideological "diversity core" has at many schools become the basis on which the superstructure of the rest of a student's education rests. One college in the mountain west, for example, offered three courses to be taken in "Diverse Cultures and Critiques" so long as they cover "critiques of the Western tradition." A Midwest college has the obligatory "Cultural Diversity Requirement," which demands three courses designated "Multicultural Studies" (including Lesbian, Gay, Bisexual, and Transgender Identities); but it has no comparable requirement in American history or Western civilization. An upper Midwest research university has first-year students take at least three required courses—including Diversity and Social Justice, The Environment, and Global Perspectives—but nothing in English literature, philosophy, or a foreign language. And, lest students consider these compulsory diversity courses as just another hurdle to jump in earning a degree, another college in the heartland sermonizes thusly: "We exist within a history of systemic cultural, political and economic oppression and privilege. In the Domestic Diversity portion of the requirement, students examine the ways groups define themselves and have been defined within this context. The groups addressed in this requirement are usually identified in terms of race, gender, sexual orientation, class or ethnicity." Happily, students will soon learn to "explore theories of race, gender, sexual orientation, class, ethnicity or other socially constructed categories."*

Where the old liberal arts tried mightily to introduce students to inquiries as far-ranging as what constitutes great literature, the history of political thought, comparative religion, or the various components of what might be called human nature, much has been reduced to a fixation on matters of race, sexuality, and privilege. Perhaps an "Introduction to Queer Studies" can serve as an intro to the liberal arts, or "The History and Practice of Whiteness in the United States." Or how about taking a course that touts "fighting racism, patriarchy, and capitalist exploitation...Field trips required"?† Perhaps, if one wants to avoid these doctrinaire studies but can't find a suitable course on, say, American history or Twain or Shakespeare, a new student might enjoy a first-year seminar called Comics and the Art of Graphic Storytelling. (It might not be a serious introduction to

---

* These examples have been culled over the years from the catalogues of Earlham College, Colorado College, Oberlin College, and the University of Minnesota. My intent is *not* to single out these schools for rebuke. They employ and offer, I trust, good professors and some instructive courses, but they also exemplify how clearly ideological their basic offerings have become. And they are not alone.

† "Fighting"—not, say, "understanding"—seems to be the implicit and often explicit aim of these courses. That is, of course, a clue to the casual reader that indoctrination has taken over from education.

serious literature, but compared to "Queering Sex Education" it sounds downright refreshing.*)

At times the debate over whether there should be some foundational core that helps begin a person's collegiate liberal arts education takes a surprising but revealing turn. I remember a debate I was part of at a Modern Language Association convention on the question of the preservation of a core curriculum, where an outspoken and well-regarded academic feminist declared herself to be in favor of some old books remaining in the core! From the audience of true believers came stunned silence, stares, a few hisses. In fact, she continued, she was in favor of the Bible remaining in every university's core. Louder hisses; some boos; astonished looks all around. "Why?" she asked. So that every student could be taught the foundations of religious fanaticism and the source of Western patriarchal oppression! Smiles, laughter, and wild, happy applause. Of course—why else would anyone study the Bible?

How sad that what began as a plea for diversity now lives as constant sameness. So much stems from a shared feeling of grievance, a shared view of the repressive nature of America or the injustice of capitalism, that a homogeneity of outlook permeates so many of their courses and offerings. For all its attachment to "criticism," the multicultural movement is amazingly uncritical. That the West is racist, sexist, and the source of continued oppression is presumed. That its malevolence stems from its peculiar cultural character is also simply assumed. That such things as gender and race are "social constructs" is a given. That thought has no independent status, that ideas are derivative, and that reason is the handmaid of the dominant power relations of society are presupposed. That culture, not

---

* All these courses in quotes are taken from the most recent Oberlin catalogue.

nature, governs all and that power governs culture—all this is simply, to them, fact. *How far this narrow and repetitive vision is from the riches and complex intellectual ferment of an older, truer liberal education is almost beyond calculation.*

Liberal education is no longer the attempt to understand the complexity of the universe and our own place in the cosmos, or even to understand our own civilization or truly learn about other cultures. It is no longer the introduction to the excitement of good novels and the ability to be moved or even transformed by the beauty of fine poetry. It is, instead, a type of badgering of incoming students, feeding them not questions but prescribed answers. It offers not thinking or support for wondering but little more than the numbing dreariness of contemporary collegiate ideology.

{10}

The Stigmatization of the Ordinary

We might think, in our professorial way, that the rejection of the high—the disparagement of great artists, serious thinkers, and wonderful writers—is without a doubt the worst thing that our colleges and universities have done. But if we want to measure the decline of the liberal arts in the *public* imagination, we might want to focus on the stigmatization of the ordinary instead of the high.

What I mean is this: Along with the political denigration of what had always been regarded as the peaks of humane learning and the literary and philosophic achievements of the West, there were other attacks and erosions. These stemmed from the view that it is not merely the highest expressions of our culture that need to be toppled but this culture's more ordinary manifestations—its "bourgeois values," the common views of right and wrong held by ordinary citizens, their everyday questions and concerns, their pride in their country, and the ethics promoted by conventional Western religious understandings. Regularly, it was not that these views would be "examined" and certainly not that they would be "understood." More often the agenda was that they would be overthrown.

In this regard, let us remember what happened to Dr. Larry Summers.

Professor Summers, president of Harvard, sparked a furor at an academic conference when he questioned the factuality of the prevalent view that the paucity of female professors in science and engineering at elite universities is the result of discrimination on the part of these universities. He then compounded his sin by mentioning that possible innate differences between men and women might be one reason fewer women seem to succeed in math and science careers. For this, the ill-fated Dr. Summers was criticized in a few places, was condemned and vilified in others (compared, indeed, to Josef Mengele in one blog), and ultimately had to resign as president of Harvard after a faculty vote of no confidence was carried against him. So entrenched, so ferocious are the politically correct partisans that simply asking certain questions—questions the PC crowd demands are closed—can bring sanction and disgrace, even to the president of Harvard.

Still, President Summers was brought down not because he said something ferociously nasty but for saying something almost anyone might ask. Unless we believe that there are no natural differences between women and men, it might seem perfectly reasonable to ask if those differences extend to interest or aptitude in math and science. If the more compelling answer is no, then we could well wish that the Harvard faculty would say so and explain why. Clearly, the ordinary and the everyday are under attack as much as greatness—great books, powerful ideas, the finest literature, notable explorers and statesmen.

This may be the deepest issue with political correctness and the root of so much widespread dissatisfaction with the liberal arts today. The problem is not that political correctness stops racist speech or ethnic slurs but that, under its sway, *the most ordinary things—ordinary questions, ordinary views—are disdained, ridiculed, and often condemned.* That people shouldn't be judged on the basis of race has surely become or is becoming a commonplace, ordinary, standard view. Except on many college campuses, where race-based affirmative action and preferencing is often the rule and where "anti-racist" curricula and procedures are in force—where the solidification of group identities and the ever-present view of American society as a battle between oppressors and the oppressed are what pass for an understanding of our principles and our history.

Consider what has become all the rage in schools and colleges around the country; consider critical race theory, the 1619 Project, and today's obsessive focus on race and identity as well as the movement toward instituting at every level an "anti-racist" curriculum. We could, as many historians and other scholars have done, dismiss these understandings as bad history, insupportable ideology, or simply the attempt to turn education and thoughtful inquiry into another form of indoctrination. But I'd like readers to think on it further.

I firmly believe that, across the political spectrum, across all races and ethnic groupings, across all ages and conditions, the common view, the *ordinary* view, is that slavery and racism are betrayals of our founding principles of liberty and equality. I also think the ordinary American view is that merit, achievement, moral responsibility, and character are all to be assessed and assigned *according to our actions as individuals*, not by our race, ethnicity, religion, or any other form of collective identity. I believe that ordinary Americans sense that no special status, no entitlement or punishment, should be bestowed simply by virtue of identity-group membership. They may differ in dozens of ways as to how to advance these ideals, but I believe they understand that these ideals stem from our basic American principles, rooted in our founding documents, and that not to honor them is shameful.

I also believe that ordinary Americans are totally willing to acknowledge that racism and racist evils are part of our history. Tulsa happened; Washington had slaves; some aspects of racism may be or have been "systemic." We Americans have all the defects of our universal and common nature, no doubt about it. But we also know that we have been helped to be, in a way, better than our natures—coaxed by our principles and ideals to do unto others, to try to give equal opportunity to all, even to go into deadly battle singing "as He died to make men holy / let us die to make men free." All this is part and parcel of America's *ordinary self-understanding*, and I imagine no amount of badgering will move us or shame us to say otherwise.

No educator should deny or paper over our shortcomings as a people. But the substitution of a simplistic view of America as "systemically" racist, or of the majority culture—including our students' parents, aunts, and uncles—as racist oppressors, or of American ideals as mere hypocrisy at best or a cover for racial subjugation at worst is easily detected as what it is: political indoctrination, not education, and a vehicle to dismiss our principles, ideals, and history out of hand rather than to look candidly at them. It is to take our students' (and their parents') ordinary sentiments of patriotism and family devotion, and their belief that our shortcomings result not from our principles but from our failure to live up to our principles, and leave these sentiments and beliefs not only rejected but, perhaps worse, *unexamined*.*

---

* This means that we should be wary of trying to forbid teaching CRT or the 1619 curriculum or any other form of racial indoctrination *by law*. Rather, the law (if it gets involved at all) should encourage schools to teach more broadly and deeply—to understand what it was that the Founders were trying to accomplish,

I do believe that those on the fringe left who see racism everywhere and those on the fringe right who would *like* to see it everywhere will fail. But what they will accomplish is to drive another nail into the coffin of liberal education. If History becomes the constant harping on all that's wrong with America, if Literature becomes the search for hidden oppression, if Religious Studies become the cataloguing of humanity using the idea of the divine to support misogyny, homophobia, and slavery, then the flight from the liberal arts will be complete.

Let's take this review of how colleges are handling matters of race and other varieties of "identity" a step further. Do you think breaking down rather than solidifying racial, gender, and ethnic barriers would be a fine, normal thing? Do you think identity politics has scant place in the search for truth or the life of the mind? Then be careful of the University of Iowa, where there's not only an Office of Equal Opportunity and Diversity and a Center for Diversity and Enrichment but also an Office of Graduate Ethnic Inclusion; a Committee on Diversity; a Council on the Status of Women; an African American Council; a Council on the Status of Latinos; an Asian American Coalition; a Native American Council; a Lesbian, Gay, Bisexual, and Transgender Staff and Faculty Association; a Gay, Lesbian, Bisexual, Transgender Union; an LGB&T Resource Center—and, of course,

---

to see what follows from their principles, to understand how they understood these ideas to be a stumbling block to rather than a cover for tyranny. To have our students understand *why* this country sought to establish itself not on blood and soil, or crown and altar, but on a set of ideas, the proposition (as Lincoln called it) that "all men are created equal," and all that followed—and did not follow—from that proposition. Try, that is, to *understand* Jefferson, Lincoln, and Martin Luther King before we dismiss or ignore them. If modern theories of identity-based democracy rather than what the Founders sought to accomplish are now in the foreground, well, let the dispute between CRT's views of our founding principles and, say, Martin Luther King's begin. In this regard, appendix E, "On Jefferson," might be a place to start.

an "ombudsperson" to oversee it all.* As we saw previously, if you want to transform society to your ideology, the first thing is to undermine the philosophers, thinkers, and books that have been the props of that society. But if you truly want to transform the culture into your understanding and image, the real prize is *to transform not only the great but the ordinary.*

✳ ✳ ✳

Let me pull back for a minute and move from concentrating on racial politics on campus to looking more generally at political correctness, speech codes, and the like. There is, it would seem, no end to the desire to prevent our students from hearing, seeing, and understanding all sides, no end to the desire to force our students to believe as they, the ideologically driven, believe.

Happily, none of this authoritarianism reigns without serious pushback. The University of Chicago sent a letter to incoming students of the class of 2020, writing, in part, "Our commitment to academic freedom means that we do not support so-called trigger warnings, we do not cancel invited speakers because their topics might prove controversial, and we do not condone the creation of intellectual 'safe spaces' where individuals can retreat from ideas and perspectives at odds with their own."[†]

In saying this, Chicago was simply reiterating the report of

---

* In a more blithe way, perhaps my favorite catalogue entry is a recent inquiry by North Dakota State University, which in its "Diversity Tool Kit" (I am not making this up) asks, "Have you ever been to a gay or lesbian bar, social club, or march? If not, why not?" Universities still discourage drinking, except at gay and lesbian bars, where it seems to be encouraged, lest the administration be seen as insensitive to the demands of diversity or insufficiently attuned to the happy celebration of difference.

† Cited in Pete Grieve, "University to Freshmen: Don't Expect Safe Spaces or Trigger Warnings," *Chicago Maroon*, August 24, 2016, https://www.chicagomaroon.com/2016/08/24/university-to-freshmen-dont-expect-safe-spaces-or-trigger-warnings/.

its Committee on Freedom of Expression from January 2015. Quoting former president Hanna Gray, the report argued that "education should not be intended to make people comfortable, it is meant to make them think. Universities should be expected to provide the conditions within which hard thought, and therefore strong disagreement, independent judgment, and the questioning of stubborn assumptions, can flourish in an environment of the greatest freedom." Or, as an earlier president, Robert M. Hutchins, observed, "without a vibrant commitment to free and open inquiry, a university ceases to be a university." *

By mid-2020, approximately seventy-five colleges and universities, including Princeton, Purdue, and Johns Hopkins, signed on to the substance of the Chicago report.†

Despite the almost obviousness of those sentiments, there remain those who understand education as a vehicle of power rather than as a vehicle for inquiry. Perhaps they might prefer to side with the president of Wesleyan, who could only say that Chicago's letter to incoming students was "a publicity stunt...[a way of] not coddling students, but coddling donors." To which he added sarcastically, "Gosh, is there any doubt?"‡

Sadly, despite powerful statements from a few thoughtful university leaders, within many colleges and universities this idea of free and open inquiry stands out not because it is common but because it is increasingly rare. More and more, colleges and universities seem unabashed in proclaiming their ideology and

---

* See University of Chicago, "Foundational Principles," Free Expression, https://freeexpression.uchicago.edu/foundational-principles/.
† Not to put too fine a point on it, but there are about 1,400 accredited institutions offering four-year undergraduate degree programs. The Department of Education, which has broader criteria, lists more than 4,000.
‡ Michael S. Roth, quoted in Richard Pérez-Peña, Mitch Smith, and Stephanie Saul, "University of Chicago Strikes Back Against Campus Political Correctness," *New York Times,* August 27, 2016, https://www.nytimes.com/2016/08/27/us/university-of-chicago-strikes-back-against-campus-political-correctness.html.

their willingness to enforce their dogmas. Where previously colleges would talk about the cultivation of the intellect, we now talk instead about the protection and celebration of groups. While we would have hoped, in the past, to promote the virtues of study, hard work, perhaps respect for the intellectual and physical property of others, now we enforce the demands not of justice but—as I mentioned—of "social" justice.

✳ ✳ ✳

I want to pause here to make one matter perfectly clear. The freedom to inquire, to pursue, to understand and weigh things afresh, is central to any education befitting free men and women with free minds. And when legitimate and serious questions cannot be raised for fear that a line will be crossed and the questioner punished, then we all can see that politics and ideology have supplanted open inquiry. *But we educators need not think we have to defend all "speech," any speech, just because we rightly defend serious and open inquiry.* Although they live and grow on the basis of freedom of thought and investigation, higher education and the liberal arts in particular do not and should not have to rally to the defense of students who want to use racial slurs or hurl scurrilous comments. Neither students nor faculty have any right to slander, ridicule, or shout down others and claim they are covered by "free speech."

But, while epithets, obscenity, and even common vulgarity may well be out of bounds, the free exchange of ideas and the right to ask any serious question—and follow where the argument leads—may not be abridged. Liberal education exists to help us understand, as best we can, the truth about the universe and ourselves within it. But if we believe that protecting "diversity" means preventing students and faculty from asking serious questions—or even ordinary questions—about certain human issues for fear that offense might be taken by some or by many, or if we think our view of social justice demands that we treat our universities as seminaries inculcating the new religion of cultural awareness' or view our colleges as the new re-education camps for ethically crippled students, then again we see how the spirit of enforcing "correct" beliefs and the spirit of liberal education have become opposite.*

Perhaps I've gotten used to the fact—perhaps we've *all* gotten used to the fact—that many in the professoriat will use the classroom to promote, instill, inculcate, and propagandize their viewpoints. Some will not use their classes to help students understand, say, the various causes and possible cures for poverty or prejudice but use their lectern as a soapbox on the failings of America or Americans. Others will casually talk of, for instance, America's hypocrisy and sexism, or of the Founders' fear of democracy and their supposed callousness regarding race and slavery without any serious effort to understand what they were attempting, what they accomplished, and why (by our standards and even theirs) they sometimes fell short. Every matter of contemporary concern—race, sex, poverty, orientation—tries to find a way to exploit the liberal arts to push its own agenda. And most students know when they're not learning history, philosophy, or English but are being hectored and badgered to accept their professor's views as the whole

---

* One of the first books cataloguing the pervasiveness of political correctness and speech codes on campus was Alan Charles Kors and Harvey Silverglate, *The Shadow University: The Betrayal of Liberty on America's Campuses* (New York: Free Press, 1998). While the incidents recounted in the book are, for the most part, simply horrendous and cover all of the academy with shame, the issue of the proper relationship of freedom of speech to serious academic freedom and the quest for knowledge still needed deeper inquiry. See my review, "Freedom and Truth in Higher Education," originally published as "Truth v. Liberty: A Confusion of Priorities," *Academic Questions* 12, no. 3 (Summer 1999), reprinted as appendix D.

story. Why study history when the professor says that our past is nothing but a catalogue of racism and hypocrisy? Better to study engineering, where they don't spend so much time puffing themselves up as wiser and more moral than those who went before. Why study literature when so many writers before our time had benighted views of race and class and sex? Maybe I'll study accounting, where I don't have to get up before the class and pretend that all the founders of modern accounting were really bad people.*

So why do college presidents no longer talk about their liberal arts offerings as the crown jewel of their collegiate instruction? Perhaps it's because they no longer are.

* * *

What is being attempted in higher education is "political" in the broadest, not narrowest, of senses: Its aim is not simply to upend the course of collegiate studies, nor to convert conservatives to progressives, nor even to push every student to become a social justice warrior, but, beyond all those, *to change the culture itself*. The reformation of the academy is not an end in itself. What good is changing the program of studies at Duke or controlling the opinions and outlook of NYU students except, through them, to reform the wider culture? It is the common culture, the "dominant culture," that needs to be changed, transformed, transvalued, not just the culture of UCLA or Harvard.

This is also why multiculturalism was rarely multicultural at all but focused so intently on the West and its flaws. It was a way of taking all that was at the heart of the liberal arts tradition—the study of the works, history, and literature of the

---

* It may be true, as a former college president and friend once told me, that not only we ordinary mortals but all the major people of history had feet of clay. But, still, he didn't understand why so many historians enjoyed the role of being foot-fetishists. Perhaps nothing gives more gratification to some than the thrill of dethroning others.

West—and hammering away at them. Multiculturalism never meant, for example, a review of the condition of women in Muslim or Hindu or African societies as much as a rehashing the evils of the West. (Indeed, since looking at issues of race, class, homosexuality, foreigners, and gender relations in non-Western cultures might actually provide a modest appreciation of the West and its achievements, the lack of such wide-ranging studies comes as no surprise.) Rather than adding to the curriculum of knowledge, multiculturalism and diversity were an attack on what came to be called the "privileging" of the Western tradition or, perhaps more particularly, the Hellenic-Judeo-Enlightenment tradition.

Finally, what seemed to start as an attempt to tear down the high and exceptional—great books, high culture, the ancient and modern Hellenic/European literary and philosophic tradition—has now moved on. Having debased and degraded the high, it is now in the midst of an attempt to defeat the ordinary—ordinary family life, heterosexuality, simple love of country, traditional virtues, traditional religious habits and outlooks. To do this, universities use not only their course offerings but all the controls at their disposal—regulations, codes, freshmen orientation, residential and extracurricular student life, sensitivity training, required diversity courses, the dismantling of "the canon," and more. This is sometimes done quietly, relying more on acquiescence and acceptance than threat, though the more committed among them can, if provoked, openly turn against their own (reflect, again, on the hapless Dr. Summers).

From the start, the real goal of the multicultural movement and then the politicization of liberal learning was not simply to enrich the study of music or add to our appreciation of new poetry; the real goal was the transformation of society at every level, from high to low. In order to accomplish this goal, what previously was deemed ordinary needed now to be stigmatized.

To believe, for example, that racial preferencing has no place in institutions of learning is now considered not reasonable but racist. To entertain notions of possible differences between men and women is now not only unacceptable but sexist. To think that one might learn something of value from ancient writers is now not ordinary but elitist. To think that a survey of Western civilization should be offered in a university core rather than courses sponsored by the women's studies department or by the coalition for LGBTQA+ studies is to open yourself to charges of sexism and homophobia as well as any number of other iniquities. To hold to orthodox religious observances and beliefs, above all to believe in any standard religious/ethical framework, might put you at odds with current views regarding lifestyle "choices" and thus at odds with modern understandings of social justice. Especially be careful of any displays of old-fashioned patriotism or love of country. You may not be censured by your fellow students; often their souls are not so dead. But you can easily run afoul of the faculty and administration acting as diversity police, protecting international students from being affrighted by any display of possible student chauvinism. Along with the high, what was once regarded as normal has now been derided and jettisoned, and a new regime of belief has supplanted what was once merely ordinary.

In all this, of course, liberal education has come out the worst. Just as dogs know the difference between being tripped over and being kicked, students know the difference between being taught and being indoctrinated, know the difference between ideas examined and ideas thrust. So, despite new requirements that *mandate* a certain number of liberal arts "diversity" courses, student adherence to the liberal arts continues to drop.

* * *

One Last Note on "Social Justice"

Where once a certain kind of inquiry—trying to gain some clarity on the meaning of justice, exploring its varied forms and claims, looking into classical, Judeo-Christian, liberal, modern, and Marxist approaches and disagreements, weighing opposing arguments, and coming to our own informed conclusions—lay at the heart of a serious education, now all is predecided and handed down. The inculcation of "social justice"—and not an inquiry into the nature of justice—has become many of our colleges' overriding mission. It is as if what has always been among the most perplexing philosophic, social, moral, and political issues is now settled.

While many of the finest minds in human history have struggled to come to grips with the meaning of justice, I imagine the simple reason so many actively proselytize for their views is that today's professors and administrators know—that is, believe they know—what real justice is! That might also be why so much of the traditional philosophic core had to be abandoned—because it would show them and especially their students that they actually *do not* know what justice is, that they hold their *opinions* to be true knowledge. Then again, maybe I'm too curmudgeonly. It reminds me of when I'm confronted with a true believer telling me he's sure he understands what God wills. It's not that I don't believe God might have a will; it's just that I would rather see the evidence—and also see it in those books I'm told not to read—and then weigh the arguments for myself.

This idea of "social justice" has many faces: On the lowest level, it sometimes means the repeated attack on ordinary thoughts and ordinary language—such as saying "fireman" or "actress" or "fellowship," or referring to "sexual preference" rather than "sexual orientation." It might mean the offense of using "he" or "she" when these days the only proper word to designate a third-person singular male or female is the often confusing and always hideously ungrammatical "they."

In its fullness, social justice means affirming many of the habits and lifestyles that the vast majority of students and their families do not share. In all this, students can rarely dissent, seldom debate, and never ridicule; they can only, safely, concur.

Beyond that, social justice can include the demand for repeated apologies to the formerly oppressed, ensuring active support for their various agendas, recognizing the importance of groups rather than individuals and persons, and asserting the primacy of group identity over a common American or human character. And it promotes the most problematic aspects of identity politics on campus with its calls for preferential treatment as well as its demands that offensive speech be proscribed, disquieting ideas be left unthought and unspoken, and those books and professors who find themselves disagreeing with this new orthodoxy be banished. This indoctrination into the regime of social justice finds itself exactly on the wrong side of both academic freedom and serious education at virtually every turn.

But all this is subject to change, and no doubt will. *Social Justice*, we should remember, was the name of the anti-Semitic journal put out by the appalling Fr. Charles Coughlin in the thirties and forties. In his hands, Coughlin and others used the demands of social justice to defend society from its enemies— especially from (as he believed) the depredation of unjust Jews and other "international financiers."

The world will change. But change is only sometimes progress.

* * *

Let me sum all this up as strongly as I can. The last thirty years have seen the vandalizing of ever so much of higher education.

The supposed reformers have entered the storehouse of centuries of accumulated knowledge, torn down its walls, thrown out its books, and toppled its monuments. For all their brave talk of justice, they have carried out what has to be seen as one of the most intellectually criminal act of the ages, the modern equivalent of burning the libraries of antiquity. Today, acts that were unthinkable, unimaginable, just years ago now seem so very ordinary.

Is any of this reversible? In part, I think so. But this requires us to have a clearer idea of where we intend to go.

PART 2

Redeeming and Reconstructing Liberal Education

{ 11 }

Liberal Education
in Its Fullness

Perhaps you found it strange that a book purportedly about the demise of liberal education opens with a sympathetic review of vocational and professional education. That wasn't just politeness on my part: I really do want us to take seriously the many virtues of non-liberal education. I especially want us to think about how vocational and professional education has been able to meld—not perfectly but to a large degree—a student's private interest with a wider public benefit.

We all know how this works: Max goes to culinary school to satisfy a longing within him to be a chef. He becomes a good chef, opens a restaurant, makes good money, raises a family, and serves good food that delights and satisfies his customers. His private good—the satisfaction of his longing to be a great chef—blended directly, naturally, into a public good. Think the same about those who study accounting or engineering or medicine.

Now think about the liberal arts. Do we have a clear idea of what the private good, the individual benefits, of a liberal arts education may be to our students? Besides providing a passably decent contestant on *Jeopardy!*, how has such an education *personally* benefited our graduate? Of course, the skills gained through a liberal education may have contributed to life in a future career. But is a liberal education merely preparatory for the good stuff that comes after we're finished with it? What benefit did a liberal arts education *in itself* contribute to the happiness of an individual student who pursued a liberating program of studies?

Second, how might a liberal education also be of benefit to *more* than the recipients of it? Knowing classical literature or American colonial history might certainly bring real satisfaction to the knower. But how can these subjects compare in value to a physician's knowledge of obstetrics or pediatric oncology? How is it that an education centered in the liberal arts can ever be "of value" to the wider society—to our friends and neighbors, to our society and country, perhaps to the culture and civilization as a whole?

I understand that there's a risk we run when we ask what good the liberal arts are to society, that we play into the hands of those who have enlisted the liberal arts to ratify their own ideological views and social agendas. But that others have used the liberal arts—or, more particularly, their politicized version of the liberal arts—for ideological aims does not mean that we should not respond. That they have made the liberal arts small does not mean we cannot again make them expansive, wise, broadly useful, and (to be honest) lovely.

In examining the many tribulations that have beset the liberal arts in the first half of this book, we nonetheless touched on much that must be said in its favor. Now, in this last half, we need to pull together these various arguments and talk about the real value of a liberal education in greater detail.

But we should be clear about one thing from the beginning: My hope is to give a "tough" defense of liberal education, not a soft or sentimental one. I have no desire to opine about how the liberal arts will turn us into individuals who are more sensitive, more humane, or more sparkling. I also have no desire to pretend that a liberally educated student is a precious ornament to society. Our students may be so, or they may not. Candidly, I find most of the great writers and thinkers in the Western tradition to be rather tough-minded and challenging, rarely sentimental and not always heart-warming. This means I have never been convinced that liberal education necessarily makes one more charming or even more moral. However, I think it does hold the potential to make us smarter than we were before and more knowledgeable about things that matter. The aim of liberal education has never been softness of spirit but rather toughness of mind.

There, let that serve as a trigger warning for those who are wondering if they should read further.

Learning About and Learning From

How exactly can the liberal arts claim to be concerned with furnishing individual minds and personal understanding yet still claim that they have a wider, civic and public, value? Or how can they claim to benefit everyone even if only a select few take advantage of them?

To answer these questions satisfactorily, let's not be reactionary. By that I mean, let's not imagine some former golden age of liberal studies to which we all must return. Our attempt to revive the study of history, fine literature, and even ancient philosophy is not to ask for a return to the ways such subjects were taught "back then." In fact, instruction in the liberal arts was, for much of the past, truly dreadful. See if you don't find C. S. Lewis's characterization of every boring, pedantic class you've ever suffered through to be spot on:

When a learned man is presented with any statement in an ancient author, the one question he never asks is whether it is true. He asks who influenced the ancient writer, and how far the statement is consistent with what he said in other books, and what phase in the writer's development, or the general history of thought, it illustrates, and how it affected later writers, and how often it has been misunderstood (especially by the learned man's own colleagues) and what the general course of criticism on it has been for the last ten years, and what is "the present state of the question." To regard the ancient writer as a possible source of knowledge—to regard that what he said could possibly modify your thoughts or your behavior—this would be rejected as unutterably simple-minded.*

To use education as a vehicle for finding the truth about the world and about ourselves is the greatest good of liberal education. To understand how our studies might modify our thoughts and our behavior for the better may well be the greatest of personal goods. And to make us truly smarter about things that matter in this world holds the strong potential to be of benefit far beyond ourselves.

To reap these benefits, educators have to drop the bias against looking for wisdom wherever it might be found, drop the prejudice against looking back, and drop the self-satisfied view that what we know today, or what we were taught in graduate school, is the latest in real learning. We must, following Lewis, be open to the notion that our education can in fact help us discern what might be true from what might be false or partial. It might help us separate what we might want to make our own from other people's opinions. And we will only

---

* C. S. Lewis, *The Screwtape Letters* (London: Geoffrey Bles, 1942; New York: HarperCollins, 2001), 139–40.

truly grow in serious understanding if we begin to appreciate the difference between *learning about* and *learning from*.

Much of liberal education falls into the soft academic trap of merely "learning about." Consider the gulf between learning *about* history or philosophy or art and learning *from* those subjects. I don't mean that we should turn every book into a philosophy text. Reading for enjoyment may result not only in insight but also in sheer delight. But how much enjoyment is sacrificed, how much delight is lost, when we turn down the opportunity to see the world as a great author saw it and foolishly make "scholarly" or "academic" the natural and near infinite joy of reading?

Let me give an example. You have, over the course of many pages, dear reader, put up with my talking about my own high school experiences. But let me try your patience just a bit more. Let me expand on Lewis's admonition to stop playing pedantic games with ancient authors, or with books of moral or political philosophy, and talk about how we might more profitably read imaginative literature. Here is one of the first essays I wrote on education, published in 1988. It begins with a story from my sophomore year of high school:

> We groaned and we grimaced and we made all the ugly noises a class of high school sophomore boys could make without being sent to the principal. We did not want to read any book about some woman, a preacher, and an out-of-wedlock baby in Ye Olde New England. It was probably a stupid book. It was surely an embarrassing book. We knew we would hate it.
>
> We loved it. Hester had the kind of character we all admired—courageous, fiercely private, loyal. Roger Chillingworth was vicious, despicable. Even though the prose was old-fashioned, every word made sense; every piece fit together.

And each day we fought in class over what we would do were we Hester or Dimmesdale or Pearl.

Then, one day, we got a special treat: a guest lecturer. One of the other teachers had taken a course, a college course, just on Hawthorne. He knew everything there was to know about *The Scarlet Letter*. He told us about the various influences on Hawthorne's prose style, the man's life and times, incidents in his career that led him to write as he did, etc., etc. Our papers were to be on "The Roots of Transcendentalism" or "The Influence of Emerson" or "Hawthorne, Man of His Times" or topics of like academic weightiness. By the time he had finished, the book was effectively dead.

I want to propose a little academic heresy in the name of common sense. Contrary to all high-blown "academic" teachings, a work of literature is great not because it has relationships to other texts that need to be explored, not because it has a long pedigree of precursors influencing its writing, not because it reveals to us ever so much about its time and place, and not because its author is a fit study for numberless biographical or psychological musings. Great literature is great because it talks about great things. And our first task as teachers is not to hide this truth, not to reduce it, not to minimize it. Our first task is to let the books we teach speak openly to our students. In some quarters, this view rubs against the grain of high scholarship. Surely it flies in the face of views that hold that all literature is merely a covert vehicle of class bias, or that there is nothing objective in texts, or that a text is whatever we make it to be, or that no one interpretation can be superior to any other. Luckily, these ideas are believed only in select universities and have not yet had much of an impact on schools.*

---

* This last comment shows how times have changed since I wrote this.

But my suggestion also means rejecting as educationally unimportant some of the rules of interpretation many of us learned when we were younger. For example, putting an author "in his time and place" may not be the most instructive thing we can do. In fact, I offer that it is positively deadly. Authors, both great and second-rate, probably can tell us more about their "historical context" than surmises about historical influences can tell us about an author. Besides, of what value is it to reduce Hawthorne or Shakespeare or Donne or Dickinson to his or her time and place? When we bind the words to their particular setting, do they mean more to us today? Are they more instructive? Generally, no.

Historical, social, or economic reductions—using history, society, or social status as an explanatory vehicle for a text—distances that text for our students. It makes it other, a curio, a museum piece. My hunch is that only second-class books are truly captives of their time; great works are more universal; they speak to us effectively as timeless. First-class works would mean no less if their authors were known only as "anonymous" and their date listed as "unknown."

There is, in other words, a sure point at which much that passes for scholarship is a kind of smug pedantry that simply kills literature. Our students, of course, know that.

As students, we knew that *The Scarlet Letter* wasn't written for us to guess at who influenced the author. We knew it wasn't about the historical context or the climate of opinion of the times when Hawthorne wrote. It was about devotion and hypocrisy and fear of being found out. It was about evil and sin and loyalty. It was about community needs, community standards, and the demands of conscience. It was about the different and conflicting parts of the human soul.

Hawthorne raised these issues of character and morals not in the context of a treatise or essay but in a novel, a particular work of art. In it, all the devices of literature come into play: What is the connotation of the rosebush outside the prison door? Why the contrast between the city and the forest? Why is the child named "Pearl"? Any question that helps us see more clearly what the story or poem or play is attempting to say to us is legitimate inquiry. Anything that pigeonholes, caricatures, reduces, or diminishes the text is not. Even as students we sensed deep down that Hawthorne didn't write to be analyzed—he had something to say and he wrote to be understood.

I am reminded of an incident that took place a few years ago at the National Endowment for the Humanities. We were trying to set up a summer school program for teachers. We hoped to reintroduce teachers to those seminal books they read, or wished they had read, when they were in school— Homer, Shakespeare, Tolstoy, de Tocqueville. Each seminar would be led by a noted college professor. The classes would center on reading one major work thoroughly. They would not be concerned with secondary sources, the latest scholarly articles on the topic, or anything that would detract from an open and careful reading of the primary text.

During the orientation session, it was clear that one of the professors was uncomfortable with the format. No, we told him, he could not assign his various articles interpreting the text for class. No, we did not think it necessary to spend much time on the historical context of the work. No, we did not want the teachers to do extensive research into the scholarly literature written about the text. In desperation, he threw up his hands and said, "But after they read the book, what will they do with it?" He simply had no idea that, with the greatest books, we don't do anything to them; they do something to us.

Along these lines, let me suggest something frightening and liberating: Do not be afraid of naïve questions. Why does

Othello kill Desdemona? Why is Iago so hateful a creature? Why does Jim trust Huck? Why does Huck never betray Jim? Why is Lear so foolish? Why does Cordelia still love him? These are the questions that live embedded in our books, embedded in ways that move both the heart and the mind. These are the reasons the author wrote. No matter what else we do, we should do the author the honor of asking what it is he or she was trying to say. If I could sum it up in one short rule, it would be this: We should all try to learn from books, not just about books.

This is a plea for taking literature seriously. It assumes that authors have something to say; even, perhaps, something to teach. It also begins with the view that great literature is always new, always contemporary, always relevant—that it can transform our view of ourselves and the world. But it can only do this if we approach our books fresh—as if they were written today, and for us. We must ask, as naïvely as we can, "Why does our author say this?" And then we should listen for reasons, not search for impersonal causes in the Zeitgeist or the subconscious or the irrational. Yes, Wordsworth is a great poet. But he's great because he has something to say, and in a manner worthy of our attention—not because he's a good example of Romanticism.

If we begin with the sense that each book, poem, or play we teach contains something relevant and worth our learning, then each encounter is the chance to grapple with the soul of a great author. Learning all "about" an author can make us feel academic, smug, and ever-so-smart. Learning all we can "from" our authors will help us see again that Hester Prynne can still talk to sophomores.*

* Originally published as "Getting the Most Out of Literature," *Basic Education* 33, no. 2 (October 1988). It was dedicated to Cleanth Brooks.

Yes, we can learn a near infinite amount *about* Shakespeare and Hawthorne or Pascal and Newton and Jefferson. But unless we are willing to look back and try to make their minds live in ours, to have their ideas and reasons inform our understanding, to have their imaginations spark our imaginations, we will have wasted far too much of our time.*

---

* You may have noticed here, and will also see in what follows, that I tend *not* to view the benefits of the liberal arts in terms of "critical thinking." Properly understood, critical thinking is not a half-bad approach to liberal learning; I just wish it were "properly understood" more often than it is. See chapter 15.

{12}

Looking Backward

As we all sense, while other parts of collegiate learning are for-ever attempting (often with success) to leap forward, traditional liberal education has a different aspect. While not expecting that our students will live in the past, we do often ask that their studies begin in the past and understand the past. But if this form of education is ground so firmly in traditional learning, how exactly can it look to be useful to the present? How can it teach so little about medicine, finance, computers, or pop culture and still have any claim to relevance? And how can it be that a liberal education, which wants to be so liberating, so freeing, always seem to be foisting on us old books, long-dead philosophers, and that most boring of subjects—history?

Think of what an imaginary student might say: "Old music? We like *our* music. Old books and plays? Wouldn't it be more interesting to read stuff written today about things going on now? Old thinkers, long-gone philosophers? Haven't we advanced since then? They may have been great in their day, but haven't we made progress, *lots* of progress, since those olden days of yore?"

All of us who teach know students who think this way, even if they don't say it this way. We know that these sentiments form a large part of the modern critique of the liberal arts: We are a progressive people, and our children should be helped to look forward, not enticed to turn around.

This is rarely an accusation leveled at us by our friends in what we often think of as the more "progressive" fields of commerce, technology, and science. Very often they know what we're doing and seem to have a modicum of respect for it. Rather, often our most serious antagonists are those in the once-standard and now reformed disciplines basic to the liberal arts themselves—literature, philosophy, history, and classics.

Still, we respond: This turning around is not a form of slavery to the past but, perhaps paradoxically, an openness that will help carry us into the future. As was said at the beginning of this book, the liberal arts are a liberation that helps lead us from opinion into greater knowledge—a liberation from what today "everybody knows" and a liberation toward what might be good or true in itself. A liberation, that is, from thinking we know, even—especially—when we do not.

Seen in this way, liberal arts become the vehicle to carry us ahead, not simply against the winds of public opinion, prejudice, or fashionable "politically correct" views but against the stifling forces of academia itself: forces that often pretend that nothing in the past can be of all that much moral or intellectual value today.

What shall we learn by looking back? How they dressed or what they ate? Some things about their "time and place"? Who influenced their thoughts or who followed those thoughts? Interesting enough, I guess, but not all that valuable.

Reflecting on what we've already noted, I can name two things we can learn. First, we learn what is ours. We understand with increased clarity the ground from which our current culture and current problems grew. What, for instance, could possibly lead Lincoln to say that the real question is not whether democracies can be established but, rather, whether they can endure? What did he—and Madison and Tocqueville—see as both the real promise and the deepest problems of democratic life? Despite what the smug among us try to teach, the past was not all prejudice and unthinking convention. Indeed, the ground of all we might take for granted today was often sharper when our way of life was new, when it needed to be rationally argued for and defended against entrenched opposition.

Second, along with knowing with greater depth and clarity what is our own, the other value of the liberal arts is giving us the minds of those whose views and insights are different, even profoundly different, from our own. Perhaps Aristotle's view of the naturalness of political life can teach us something about the radicalness as well as the limits of modern Lockean/Jeffersonian individualism. Perhaps Thucydides's expansive view of human nature, hubris, courage, and the problem of piety can give us a richer view of how to approach political life and its challenges than, for example, today's shallow slogans about whether government or economics is the problem or the solution.

If human nature doesn't change all that much over time, if it's possible that good and evil exist independent of societal customs, if the matters and madness of the human heart seem to be as much ancient as modern, why would we willingly cut ourselves off from learning wherever we can?

In this light, the great paradox of the liberal arts becomes clearer: In possessing the minds of the finest writers, artists, and thinkers, we do something that is both backward-looking and simply, totally, progressive. We can see the roots and reasons for what we call our own and be liberated from believing that we and our peers—or even our parents and professors—have the latest corner on human wisdom. That is, by trying to grasp the minds of the finest thinkers and writers who have lived, we might, for the first time, come to possess our own minds.*

A Note on Magic

I've just argued that among the wonders of the liberal arts is the knowledge that through our study of these arts we might *possess the minds* of great but long-dead authors and thinkers, that we might attempt to make their minds live in ours.

One might be shocked by that formulation, since at first blush it appears to be some kind of mystical claptrap. But if there's any truth to it, it is clearly something wonderful, marvelous—nearly magical.

Let me have recourse once again to Aristotle. I freely admit that Aristotle has been, for me, first impenetrable, then difficult, but is now a serious and happy part of my intellectual life. Along with Socrates, Shakespeare, Galileo, and Newton, Aristotle is an intellect of towering genius, a genius with whom I have tried, over years, to come to terms. But "coming to terms" with Aristotle has meant reading, asking him questions, getting exasperated, then making him into someone with whom I can have a conversation. In time, old Aristotle became to me, and to many of my colleagues, a friend.

When you consider it, this is surpassing strange. Aristotle is dead. In a real way, extremely dead. But, in a more important way, hardly dead at all. You see, *the most immaterial thing about him turns out to be the most permanent and solid thing about him*: his mind.

People may want someone else's features or strength; we

---

* To exemplify this, I've taken the case of Thomas Jefferson, whose life and writings are not only central to our American self-understanding but—as they have always been—deeply controversial. See appendix E.

may want something physical and bodily. But we can never really possess someone else's material body even with the best of medical science at our disposal. We can, however, have the part of him or her that's *not* material. We can possess someone else's mind. Aristotle's body has been a-moldering in the grave for millennia, but his ideas and reasoning—his mind—can live forever in us because he wrote and we have learned how to read.

Thus, by reading today but looking back, we can possess the mind of perhaps the greatest genius who ever lived. Is this not the magic, the stupendous magic, of the liberal arts?

{ 13 }

Wonder and Longing

The reason the philosopher can be compared to the poet is that both begin in wonder.

—Thomas Aquinas, *Commentary on Aristotle's "Metaphysics"**

I mentioned in a previous chapter my the fictive student "Max," who longed to become a great chef, went to culinary school, and followed his dream. Though we all might share a common human nature, we also know that our dreams and longings are hardly uniform. That said, while we can easily understand what aspects of human desire might lead a person to want to be a chef or soldier or even a long-haul trucker, what longings lead students to immerse themselves in the liberal arts? Here's a beginning.

Aristotle famously tells us that all people desire to know. Undergraduates regularly scoff when they run across this, as if the Philosopher had said that all people desire to study or do homework or go to graduate school. But Aristotle saw what I think we all sense as well—each and every one of us longs to know, truly know, thousands of things.

Animals, it would seem, rarely ask questions; but people always do. Most of us want to know what's ours and what's not ours. Many of us want to know about God or the natural

---

* I am indebted to Josef Pieper's penetrating essay "The Philosophical Act" (1952) for connecting this idea not only to philosophy but to the study of all the liberal arts.

order—Does God exist? What does He want of me? And does He actually punish and reward? Reflecting on our lives and the lives of others, we might ask what part do genetics or self-interest or culture or reason or ignorance play in our actions. Some of us want to know as much as we can about great art, or how to tell the just from the unjust, or what makes cultures different, or how to understand the laws of physics.

Now, not all that we long to know is so "philosophical." We regularly want to know the answer to more mundane though still quite important questions: How do I make a soufflé? What's the best way to get from Chicago to Philadelphia? But keep in mind that some questions that might seem at first mundane are so much more: What should I look for in a husband or a wife? How can I be a good friend to my neighbor? What, moreover, does "being a friend" or even being a "neighbor" really mean?

It is interesting that the most important questions often come to us fully answered. Our culture, our faith, our tribe, and our family all package up for us ready answers to the most central human questions. One might be tempted to say that in the quest for knowledge, knowledge we try to make our own through reason and reflection, we always stumble over at least five Ps—parents, patriots, priests, peers, and professors. But, without disrespect, we in the liberal arts are pressed to respond by saying, "You might be right, but I really do need to see for myself, to learn for myself. I need to see the reasons for things, to understand them as best I can. I might even need to find out if what you tell me is true. I need to know if your answers are all there are or if there are other answers, better answers, or perhaps no answers that I can reach." This is not cynicism, nor is it arrogance. It simply means that real education necessitates that the quest for understanding should not be foreclosed.

Living simply in the cave of opinion can be comforting, and living and thinking as others do is easy. But there are students, often our best students, who long to know more, who have serious questions that go far beyond mere opinions and want to know the world in as much of its fullness and marvel as they can absorb.

For such students, the pursuit of the liberal arts begins in two interconnected parts of their being: (1) their mind as it wonders, marveling at our strange and stupendous world so full of desire, fear, hope, and uncertainty, and (2) their heart, which houses the serious desire to know better the truth about those questions that contain our deepest longings.

Indeed, the list of what we often long to understand might often seem nearly infinite; but it may be instructive to write down a few:

- Who am I? Why am I? Does my life—do our lives—have a purpose, or is human life random, unnoticed in the larger scheme of things, unrewarded and unpunished?
- What should I do to be a good person? *Why* should I want to be a good person? And what do we really mean by the words "good person"? Is it best actually to be good or is it enough to be thought of as good?
- Does the universe have a creator? If it does, does he care? Why do we seem so eager to think that God is a person, whether he or she?
- Why do we humans seem to love peace but are so often at war? Might war be natural and permanent?
- What makes something beautiful? Noble?
- I'm told that all we need is love, but I'm not sure I know what love is. I imagine it's a kind of "devotion,"

but I also know that people can be devoted, fanatically devoted, to some terrible and deadly things. Why is love so problematic?

- As I wonder what should be the objects of my devotion, what, if anything, should I hate? What should I rightly hold in contempt?
- I wonder if it's true that "all men are created equal." What do those words even mean?
- As we look with marvel at the universe, does not Pascal also speak for us when he admits "the eternal silence of these infinite spaces terrifies me"?

While we're on the topic of questions, we should note that there have always been a few in the liberal arts who see the asking of questions as pretty much an end in itself. I've even heard it said that there are no interesting answers, only interesting questions. But what could be less satisfying than that? We ask questions, honest questions, because we truly do want to have the best answers we can find. Clever questioning might show our associates how smart and sophisticated we think we are; but wondering, real wondering, can never really be satisfied with sophistication.*

Let me here offer a simple set of categories where the liberal arts can help us in our desire to know, can help us

---

* But, as we talked about when discussing liberal education and ideology, today the often more prevalent stance is not one that prefers questions over answers but one that privileges pat answers and ideology over real inquiry. Again, true teaching is helping our students see what the important questions are and what the variety of important answers might be. Not what *our* answer is; not what the answers of today's supposedly most just or sensitive or socially aware people are; but what the range and scope of all serious answers might be. This is also why I'm not sure that freedom of *expression* is necessarily at the core of academic life—but freedom of *inquiry* most certainly is.

satisfy our wondering. We study history, we read great books, we delve into literature, we study cultures and religious traditions, we fall in love with fine art and great music for all kinds of wonderful reasons. Often, it's for entertainment and delight, or to understand the natural world and its marvels, or to consider why we as a civilization are the way we are and how we differ from other cultures. But perhaps the most important reason for liberal learning, even more than to understand what's ours and not ours, is to learn what is *universal*. To discover what makes us human is the highest and most philosophical aspect of wondering. And we can glimpse the answers we seek not only through philosophy but also through literature and poetry, religious and classical studies, history, and all the liberal arts.

Given that, let's propose a definition of the liberal arts that goes beyond listing the academic subjects it might contain or the kinds of questions it hopes to help us answer. Consider this: *The liberal arts are a way of understanding the most important questions of human concern through reason and reflection.* That is, through wondering, followed by reading, thinking, and questioning.

Now it's surely true that over 90 percent of all we know we have not reasoned to on our own or learned through study. We take the word of others all the time. We could hardly live in society without doing this, and we do it naturally. I take it on the word of others that not all mushrooms are edible; I accept that certain acts—say cruelty, murder, incest, theft, and hundreds of others—are wicked. I believe, without serious examination on my part, that the earth isn't flat and that it revolves around the sun. I know that humanity has, over centuries and centuries, pondered these questions and in most cases come up with good answers. But I also know that these answers—let's say that the earth revolves around the sun and that murder is evil—came about through *reflections* on nature and reflections on the nature of right and wrong. And while we take many questions of human concern as settled, there was a time when the answers to these questions were new, when killing those outside of our tribe was not merely allowed but often encouraged, when literally everyone thought the sun went around the earth. That we all take so much on faith as we live our lives is both true and necessary. But it doesn't mean the longing to know *why*, if that longing exists within us, should ever be let go. It's such a longing to know that has refined the world's given answers and moved us forward.*

So the first and perhaps most important reason why the young are sometimes deeply attracted to the liberal arts is that there's a kind of burning within them that cannot easily be satisfied with pat answers. Yes, non-liberal but still worthy fields may often attract them more. Yes, there's always the allure of money that the study of the liberal arts cannot promise. Yes, they might be turned off by bad or partisan instruction. But there will always be many, very many, who are forever inquisitive, who view the world with wonder—even astonishment—who so thirst to know the truth about God or man or the natural world that they can only be satisfied with knowing more. This is also why the liberal arts have always found a home in high schools and colleges: to meet the young at the age when the desire to know what great literature might offer, or to comprehend the beautiful, or to see for ourselves what justice or duty or devo-

---

* How odd it is that the most progress seems to have come in answering our questions about the world of "things," about the order of the natural universe, and how perplexed we still are about so many *human* things—about the just and unjust, about religion, about human nature, about ourselves. This is why common opinion is important for everyday life and also why it is important to ask it to make an account of itself.

tion might demand—to meet the young when the desire truly *to know* burns in them most brightly.*

---

* I was, as I noted, a graduate student at Cornell in the late sixties and early seventies, and I studied political philosophy with Allan Bloom. When the university was besieged by radicals who, bluntly, took it over and shut it down, Mr. Bloom seemed rather unfazed. Indeed, he seemed to me always to keep lines of communication and discussion open with the leaders of the SDS. When some of us questioned him about this, he said, yes, in their fanaticism they did a truly great crime—they closed down a world-class university. But still, these were students in whom the desire to know what justice was burned the hottest. Which meant that he—or he and Plato and Rousseau—could reach at least some of them. Many other professors in history or government were recipients of death threats, but I don't believe Mr. Bloom ever was.

⟨14⟩

Universals and Particulars

I understand how "elevated" the previous chapter might seem. While knowledge of the truth about matters of universal concern is central to the study of the liberal arts, the liberal arts aren't always and everywhere so philosophic in their reach. Literature contains truly good books and not simply Great Books, books that may entertain as well as instruct. Shakespeare's *Henry V* may teach much about courage and loyalty. But it also is a gripping war story and a play replete with high oratory, intrigue, and love. *The Odyssey* might still be the best story about adventure and fantastic tales, as well as inviting us to think about the true meaning of fidelity and home. And what of *Alice in Wonderland* or *Brave New World* or *The Heart of Darkness* or the short stories of Flannery O' Connor or even *The Secret Life of Walter Mitty*? These and literally thousands of others lay out before the reader stories of humor or horror, perhaps romance or despair, pity or mystery. Even so light a book as *Penrod and Sam* gave us young teenage boys insight into what it meant to be imaginative and showed us that we could be imaginative ourselves.

Moreover, did the first half of this book talk not simply about universals but, more particularly, about knowing our own and understanding something of what was *not* our own? I want to return to that framework since I want us to think about a liberal arts education in the context of America and also begin to point in the direction of understanding the liberal arts as a public benefit as well as a private blessing.

So let's return to the matter of the study of Western civilization and America.

Within the broad culture of the West, America holds a particular place. We have, first, the culture of Western civilization itself—Athens, Rome, Jerusalem; Homer, Genesis, and the Gospel of John; Shakespeare, Mozart, Vermeer, Picasso; the Middle Ages, the Crusades, the Renaissance, the Reformation, and the global expansion of the West. From that, and in addition to it, we have the particular culture of America—from the Declaration of Independence and the Constitution to Lincoln and the Civil War to Jim Crow and the civil rights movements to the tortured politics and "culture" of today. Even the finest liberal arts education will introduce us to only a small portion of the immensity of our Western/American civilization.

But where to begin—and what might we hope to learn? Thinking back to what we said earlier, let me propose that the first reason to learn about Western civilization and its American annex is not because it is good (parts are, but parts are not) or true (some surely are, some not) or eternal (it is not) but because it is *ours*. Ours *together*. Our principles, our outlook, our beliefs, our institutions—including everything from political institutions to colleges and universities to hospitals to the organization of the family. All have been built up by this construct we call Western/American civilization.

If the first aim of a true education is Socrates's dictum that we should know ourselves, then any person—male or female, white or Black, poor or rich—who is unfamiliar with the Bible or with our ancient stories, fables, and myths, who is unacquainted with the broad outlines of the history of Europe or of the reasons for the Reformation, or who has never read any Shakespeare or heard any Mozart will be lost in this culture. He or she will know little of the forces and ideas that shaped the daily life of every one of us on every level.

Note that without some real, broad, and systematic exposure to the works of this culture, our students, including minority students and children of recent immigrants, will have been cheated. They will be kept as strangers in a strange land. Without knowledge of the ideas and history (both comfortable and uncomfortable) of this civilization, there will be little empowerment because there will be little understanding of the things that surround and impinge on their daily lives. But mostly their *minds* will have been cheated: If they leave school not knowing some portion of the great literature of this culture, or what our finest art and architecture looks like, or what our great music sounds like, they are seriously *cheated*. This culture is their culture. They have every right to know it.*

But, some may rightly add, America is different. We are the most diverse and multicultural part of Western civilization, without exception. Because we are diverse, for each of us "our own" means not only what we hold in common but also what we hold separately. If the principle that "knowing one's own" is legitimate and necessary to be educated, then it is true

---

* To be blunt, the corollary of this is that it is simply more important—initially—for an American to know the Declaration of Independence and the Gettysburg Address than to know the principles of Eastern mysticism. It is, conversely, more important for recent Asian immigrants to know who Martin Luther King was than for American Blacks to know the names of great figures in Cambodian politics. This isn't arrogance on the part of Americans or on the part of other cultures when they do the same. It is simply a recognition that education is meant to make the culture (before some students are pushed to disdain or reject it) somewhat understandable.

for Blacks and Hispanics as well as whites, Asians as well as Italians, Catholics and Jews as well as Protestants. *As long as the invitation to understand the broader culture is seriously offered,* there is nothing remiss in Catholic students studying Catholicism or African American students wanting to know more about Black history and Black literature or Chinese students taking courses in Asian culture. The coexistence between the common and the particular has always existed in this most multicultural and diverse of countries—so long as the common culture is truly offered for transmission and not trashed in the promotion of particularism.

{15}

The Delight of Wondering and the Critical Stance

"Of course, I should have been an artist myself," said the Critic,
"if I had not seen through the whole business so clearly."
—THOMAS MANN, *THE INFANT PRODIGY*

There's a tension at the core of liberal learning that may be growing more and more apparent. On one hand, we've talked about the liberating aspirations of a well-conceived program of liberal arts studies—the movement from opinion and common prejudices to something closer to truth, the growing possession of our own minds and the freeing of our imaginations, the moving from the dark cave of opinion and myth to seeing things as they truly are. On the other hand, we've also criticized that kind of liberal arts education that has little but contempt for common opinion, a kind of haughtiness that delights in "stigmatizing the ordinary." We have praised freedom of inquiry while also defending respect for the past, the preservation of tradition, and the serious reading of old books.* We expect the liberal arts to move us forward as well as remind us to look back.†

---

* "Freedom of inquiry" is a better phrase than freedom of speech or, especially, freedom of "expression." Inquiry—careful, serious, and analytic thought—is at the heart of higher education; speech, or mere "expression," less so. (Do I need to explain this? No, of course not.)

† The first task—to be the defender of free inquiry—the liberal arts share fully with all the various colleges and departments that make up our institutions of higher learning. The second—the transmission of the great tradition of civilized learning—pretty much has fallen to our schools and colleges of liberal arts, who, sadly, seem trying mightily to abandon this task.

139

That the liberal arts may well have both a liberal—liberating—side and a conserving and tradition-preserving side is, I believe, the simple truth. A superior liberal arts education can liberate us to think for ourselves while it offers the greatest art, books, plays, and ideas that have been cultivated and refined over almost 3,000 years to help us think. Not only are both aspects of liberal education, the liberating and the conserving, justified in themselves, but they also need and support each other.

While the conserving nature of the liberal arts is easy enough to grasp, we probably need to say at least one more thing about the liberal arts and freedom. I'm somewhat cautious of the movement to equate the freedom to question and to be skeptical, inherent in liberal education, with "critical thinking" or, even more radically, with "subversive education."

I understand the desire to turn the liberating arts into the subversive arts because, much to my chagrin, I fear I've spoken of liberal education too much like that in the past. I would say to incoming students that the goal of a great liberal education is to question everything, hold all ideas up to relentless criticism—to act as Socrates did and puncture pretense and prejudice at every turn. In the pursuit of moving from the cave of superstition and mere opinion, inching closer to the light of truth, relentless questioning is our task. We are to be radical thinkers in the most fundamental—fundamentalist—way.

This was an exhilarating—though now I believe incomplete—way of looking at the liberal arts. It was also an approach I took in part from Allan Bloom, my graduate professor in political philosophy and one of the most captivating professors anyone could ever know.* As he would say, we should see the

---

* This is the same Allan Bloom who wrote *The Closing of the American Mind* (New York: Simon and Schuster, 1987), a book praised by many traditionalists who failed to see its radicalism and excoriated by the left, who also failed to see it.

liberal arts as the solvent that dissolves convention, the hammer that smashes all idols, and the power that will liberate our minds from the tyranny of the *Ps*—especially parents, poets, and priests.*

Thus, in the hope of cultivating independent thought, students should question everything, ferret out every real or imagined contradiction, expose all supposed weak spots, and, perhaps above all, shame hypocrisy. Isn't this, we are told, what Socrates did?

I can understand and defend this impetus toward "radical questioning" if what we seek is to have our authors and our texts explain to us their meaning, their reasons, their most powerful arguments. I also understand it if the idea is to hold up contemporary life by comparing it to other ways of life, looking at the most basic and serious arguments both sides make.

But too often radical questioning isn't so much an attempt to ask serious questions to get to the heart of a position or elucidate the reasons why something is believed—in the hands of a politicized professoriat, all too often it is a way not of learning but of dismissing.

---

* See Bloom, *Closing*, 119, where the formulation is "family, faith, [and] country." Also see 254 (on being "contemptuous of public opinion"); 258 (on reason as "necessarily subversive"); 274–78 (on the conflict between the liberal arts and civic life); and 370, "true liberal education requires that the student's whole life be radically changed by it…Liberal education puts everything at risk and requires students who are able to risk everything."

Why "poets"? First, because the finest poets were often those who sang of a people's greatness, their traditions, their "culture," and their country. Second, and perhaps more importantly, poets are songsters, and songs, including hymns, rarely philosophize. They look instead to trigger the emotions, heighten passions, praise faith, arouse, and even enflame. Socrates highlights the conflict between poetry and philosophy not because he thought poetry useless or silly but because he knew it is *extremely* powerful. We teachers and professors know this when we see the grip songs have over our students, how lyrics buttressed by sound shape their minds and sensibilities. How the liberal arts have sought to tame poetry and use it as an ally, in the pursuit not of prejudice and passion but of thoughtfulness, could be the subject of more than a few books.

As teachers, we must be careful. In saying that we in the liberal arts are essentially challengers and questioners, we also begin the shallow activity of puffing ourselves up. We think to ourselves, "We surely aren't Socrates, but if we teach our students to challenge everything, maybe we're on the way to being a pretty fair imitation."

This is a partial and self-serving view of the Socratic enterprise. To take Socrates at his word, the reason he would ask questions was to find out what people knew. It was the search for knowledge, not particularly the desire to undermine, that animated his questioning. To be certain, most of the people Socrates spoke with very often did not know all they claimed to know. Their notions of justice, piety, and morality were almost always partial or contradictory. But it was not radical doubt that pushed Socrates; rather, it was a desire to find out what people actually did know and could defend. Socrates is not Descartes. We imitate Socrates best when we ask our authors to tell us what they know and ask them to raise us up, not when we think we know what makes them tick or what motivates them or where they so obviously went wrong.

More importantly: A few chapters back we said that the liberal arts hold the promise of liberating us from prejudice and unexamined opinions. But it isn't simply the unexamined biases of *others* that we were to free ourselves from. Most of all it was *our* myths, *our* prejudices, *our* opinions, and what is so bizarrely called these days "our truth" that needed to be examined in the light of reason and through the medium of centuries of writings and arguments.

But what shall we say about that close relative of education as subversion, namely "critical thinking"? Critical thinking is in many ways the less strident younger brother of smashing all conventions or dethroning all idols. It presents itself as a milder but still serious inquiry. And I do believe that true critical thinking—thinking that understands an author as he understands himself, that sees the complexity of an event or era, that comprehends the various threads of causality and has an understanding of human motives, mixed and pure; thinking that sees in great literature the immensity of our human imaginations; thinking that has some sympathy for the various problems we humans have faced and knows that options are often limited; and, above all, thinking that tries to comprehend the reasons for this idea, this action, or this event—this understanding of "critical thinking" is truly a valid and valuable approach to liberal learning.

Perhaps this was the kind of endeavor that proponents of critical thinking meant originally. In that case, critical thinking can easily be called analytic thinking, evaluative thinking, reason-based thinking, careful thinking, or, perhaps, just simply *thinking*. Thinking that is clear, insightful, and even sympathetic—not suspicious or looking for ways to reject but in search of what truths might be found based on reasoned argument.

But that's hardly what we see around us today. Criticism and a critical stance far more narrowly conceived are ascendant. Perhaps this makes us seem closer to being true intellectuals. Liberal artists today study "literary criticism," often in preference to studying mere "literature"; we have "historical criticism" more than mere "history." Besides, doesn't being a critic make us more of a real scholar? Maybe critics and scholars are better than authors or poets or playwrights—after all, aren't they (as Thomas Mann suggests in the epigraph to this chapter) the ones who understand things at a higher (or is it deeper?) level?

All too often to read critically means to approach a text looking for biases or errors, or at how little the author knew compared to us. But think how much better it would be to approach a text as if *we* are the ones with prejudices and half-formed opinions. To see that the bias might be with us, the readers and professors. To grow in learning means that we all have to be open to that.

※ ※ ※

If we hope truly to learn I suggest we don't begin with radical questioning or trying to overturn all conventions, or with judging others on the basis of whether they support our opinions. Begin, instead, with *wonder*. That wonder, that marveling, which begins in knowledge of our ignorance and then gives rise to the desire to know more, is the beginning of the wisdom in the liberal arts. It is the wonder that ranges over all aspects of the universe, both made and natural, that leads us to ask, to seek, and to try to understand. It is that marveling even at a simple leaf of cabbage that gives rise to many of the deepest questions about the natural order—its seeming incomprehensible complexity and its equally obvious order. There's a joy of discovery in this education, of seeing things clearly and for the first time. And there's a real happiness that no other earthly creature appears able to have, of knowing how things work and why they work and the reasons and arguments behind things.

I actually think this dichotomy—between whether liberal education rests on a foundation of radical questioning and criticism or on a foundation of wonder and marveling—is not simply a minor, in-house argument but a dispute of serious consequence. In the end, both radical or subversive questioning and heightened "critical" thinking say more than they should and accomplish less than they should. They all slide too easily from critical thinking to mere criticism, winding up with all the false romance and all the dangers of nihilism. Those who believe in such a form of liberal education move from the unsupportable claim that within the liberal arts all our questions will be answered to the rather arrogant claim that, through their teaching, all answers will be questioned. Rather than encouraging students to learn all they can from our books, our authors, from philosophy, and from history, they encourage students to find what they think is weak or wrong and show it up for what it is. And so it turns the learning process upside-down—it makes the student and his thoughts (or, more often, his "feelings" and opinions) the center of inquiry and not the text, events, theories, or ideas under investigation.

We need to be clear. In one truly important way, there's nothing wrong with asking our students to be critical or, better, "evaluative." To return to my field of politics, we might urge students to articulate how they understand Lincoln's oft-stated belief that it was more important to save the union than immediately to free the slaves, or why it might be that the American Founders established a modified democracy and not a more thoroughgoing one. We should give students complete room to evaluate Lincoln's or Madison's views. But these evaluations, these items of critical thought, come after understanding, after reading and trying to comprehend Madison's and Lincoln's thoughts, after everything relevant we can know about a writer, ideas, or events. The liberal arts do not begin in criticism, as generally understood, but they can and properly do culminate in it.

✳ ✳ ✳

While I have my doubts about the justice of reducing the liberal arts to radical questioning or criticism in the usual sense of the term, I do not intend to demean or disparage questioning itself. Properly grounded questions that are not clever expressions of our untutored opinions but real questions in search of real answers are central to what it means to become educated—not questions designed to show how smart we are but questions designed to elicit serious and weighty answers, if such answers are there. Sometimes this means asking the most basic, the most puzzled, even the most naïve of questions: "Dante, why are those who betray the trust of their friends in the lowest depths of Hell and not atheists or blasphemers or even murderers of children?" "I don't understand, Shakespeare, what motivates Iago. Is he simply inhuman, or is there something of Iago in all our natures?" Or "How can it be that Shylock seems to me both merciless and sympathetic at the same time?" You see, great authors love great questions; and often the most open and most naïve questions are the truly great ones. These types of questions can elevate a lecture or, above all, make a seminar of prepared and inquisitive students sparkle.

What this means is that we who profess the liberal arts have one of the hardest but perhaps most noble of jobs—we cannot be content with being critics; we have to be open searchers after the truth.

In saying this, I'm asking that we in education go back to an older understanding of the liberal arts as the home not of sophistication but of naïveté.

Seen in this light, the highest goal of liberal education is not to overturn your mind as much as to expand it: to give it reasons where before there might have been just guesses; knowledge where there was opinion; new perspectives where there might have been blind single-mindedness; principles where there were before simply slogans. None of this stops us from being evaluative or "critical." Indeed, it points us in the direction, finally, of making judgments and having them be sound. But, as I said, this is where our intellectual life points, not where it begins.

None of this will change the mind of even one professor who thinks that deconstructing literature, debunking history, or dethroning all idols but his own is what teaching is all about. In thinking he is the new Socrates, he forgets that Socrates began with the knowledge of his ignorance, and from a wonder at what is and why it might be so. In like manner, we, too, can tell students that the purpose of a real education is to have them marvel at things they never saw before, perhaps come to a better and surer understanding of beliefs they already hold, and learn better how to think, analyze, and weigh evidence so as, in the end, to come into the possession of their own minds.*

---

* Two things: For more on literary criticism, historicism, and other ills of contemporary academic life, see appendix F, "The Politics of Reading." For more on political correctness, see my "To Reform the Politically Correct University, First Reform the Liberal Arts," in *The Politically Correct University: Problems, Scope, and Reforms*, ed. Robert Maranto, Richard E. Redding, and Frederick M. Hess (Washington, DC: AEI Press, 2009), 287–97.

{16}

On Individual Progress and the Common Good

This book began with the comparison of liberal arts education to other types of education. I wanted to look at how vocational, technical, and professional education try to satisfy the needs and desires of their students while using those studies to add to the common good of America and perhaps the world.

It was easy to show how the study of medicine or business might be of use to individuals as well as to society. But when it comes to the liberal arts, and especially the humanities, showing the *personal* benefits or the *societal* benefits of Suzie learning Latin or Joey studying poetry seemed not all that obvious. We have, to be sure, touched on these matters in many places throughout the book; now it falls to us to try to bring them all together.

* * *

So let us begin with what might be the use of a liberal education for each of us as individuals.

I've tried to show how a liberal education can help satisfy, in rich and expansive ways, the universal desire each of us has *to know*. Not to know just anything but to gain insight into our most serious questions. And how it is that a liberal education hopes to take our wondering about these questions—questions about love and fear and justice and human excellence—and discuss them with our students when these questions, and this desire to know more, burns within them most strongly.

Moreover, I've tried to show how the liberal arts, properly conceived and taught, can introduce our students to the best thinkers, authors, and artists from antiquity to the present, how it could give students exposure to what would be, for them, new ideas and perspectives, and how it can offer them the chance to think through these matters for themselves and come to their own conclusions through reason and reflection. This might cultivate the ability in them to possess their own minds, freely, even in the face of what our culture, their peers, today's ever-present "celebrities," or even their more ideological professors might think. This is among the most weighty arguments for liberal education: The freedom to think, to imagine, to question, and to dissent is part of what it means to be a free man or woman.

Moreover, it seems unlikely that freedom of thought and inquiry can be constricted without impinging on freedom more generally. If we learn nothing else from some of the books in the liberal tradition, we should see that constraining freedom of the mind today leads to control in other, perhaps all, areas of human life and flourishing later.

Still even this is not enough. I vividly remember reading in a biography of Abraham Lincoln that he ferociously studied Shakespeare, the Bible, poetry, and Jefferson not just to better understand this or that but, above all, to see what the pattern of a man's life might be like.* It was not enough for him to scan the world of learning and become more knowledgeable

---

* Lord Charnwood (Godfrey Rathbone Benson), *Abraham Lincoln* (New York: Henry Holt and Company, 1916), 11.

about many of life's most serious matters—Lincoln wanted to see what he might *be* and *do*. That is, he needed to understand better how he should live.

* * *

From these high notes of freedom, longing, and human excellence, let's drop down an octave or two. One word I've used many times in this book, and an idea that John Henry Newman, the most comprehensive writer on education, also leans on, is "ordinary." The liberal arts may do many extraordinary things, but in many ways they also do some things quite ordinary: The liberal arts are that "great but ordinary means to a great but ordinary end."* What great but ordinary things might Newman be talking about? How about learning how to read with comprehension and thoroughness. "Read?" you say. "What an ordinary thing." Yes, but when you read carefully and sympathetically (again, not exactly "critically" but sympathetically), you open the door to an amazing thing: another person's mind. In a way, an ordinary thing. And yet an immensely wonderful thing.

Consider the questions about which we hope the liberal arts might help us get some clarity: "Is there really something called justice or is it simply another preference?" "Is the universe ordered or is it merely random?" "How might I view my rights and society's needs—and how should I weigh their competing claims?" These kinds of questions might seem simple or naïve, or they might seem complex and deep. But they are in a real way quite ordinary, questions we all ask ourselves as we interact with the world and with others.

But Newman hardly leaves it there. How else might a liberal education be useful to us as individuals? Such an education helps us "to disentangle a skein of thought, to detect what's

---

* John Henry Cardinal Newman, *The Idea of a University* (1852; repr., Garden City, NY: Image Books, 1959), 191.

sophistical, and discard what's irrelevant." Such an education gives a clearer and more conscious view of our own opinions and helps us refine them. Such an education might show us "how to influence others, how to come to an understanding with them, and how to bear with them."*

None of this is in the slightest way trivial. Growing in knowledge about important matters is the purpose of a good education; remaining carelessly attached to our unexamined opinions is a mark, sadly, of ignorance.†

In overcoming our ignorance of the past through history and our ignorance of human nature through philosophy and literature, we are less likely to be ruled by slogans or unexamined opinion, less likely to be moved simply by emotion or by demagogues, perhaps even less easily duped because we lack a conception of the evil possibilities of our common natures.

This is a long list of serious expectations we might hope to gain from the study of the liberal arts. Some, such as the ability to confront our own opinions and refine them, or to untangle a mass of confusing arguments and mine them for what truths they may contain, are central to becoming truly educated. Others that Newman assumes without expanding on are the ability of books to enrich our imaginations, to teach us clarity and precision in writing, and to give us serious insight into what might be truly beautiful.

In keeping with my view that we should stop overpromising the good that the liberal arts can do, let me repeat that I'm not sure studying the liberal arts will make us better people, at least not as the world today often understands "better"—more

---

* Newman, *Idea*, 192.
† I am tempted to cite that great American philosopher John Wayne, who is reputed to have offered, "Life's hard. But it's harder if you're stupid." But I won't because it seems doubtful Mr. Wayne ever actually said it.

charitable, kinder, perhaps more caring and compassionate, or, all in all, more "liberal."

I admit that insofar as they teach us to read boldly as seekers after truth, the liberal arts can help move us closer to two old-fashioned virtues—courage, in that we invite students to grapple with some of the greatest minds and try to make them our own; and humility, in that our best students know they are seekers after truth, not yet possessors of it. But when it come to our more common understanding of virtue, I think Newman is right:

Knowledge is one thing, virtue another; good sense is not conscience, refinement is not humility...Philosophy, however enlightened, however professional, gives no command over the passions....

Taken by themselves, [the liberal arts] do but seem to be what they are not; they look like virtue at a distance, but they are detected by close observation, and on the long run; and hence it is that they are popularly accused of pretense and hypocrisy, not, I repeat, from their own fault, but because their professors and their admirers persist in taking them for what they are not, and are officious in arrogating for them a praise to which they have no claim.

Quarry the granite rock with razors, or moor the vessel with a thread of silk; then you may hope with such keen and delicate instruments as human knowledge and human reason to contend against those giants, the passion and the pride of man.*

---

* Newman, *Idea*, 144–45. If our teaching can help students write with even half the precision and elegance of Cardinal Newman's prose, we will have accomplished a truly marvelous thing.

There is, however, one attribute that a liberal education might indeed cultivate, though it is hardly counted as a virtue by many sides today—moderation. Perhaps this is the virtue a liberal education cultivates best, as well as the virtue for which it is often criticized most.

We live, as we all recognize, in a most immoderate age. Too much is passion, too much is commitment. But consider an education that encourages us and our students to look back with openness and respect for possible guidance, to look at the most important questions from many sides, to be skeptical of the biases and felt truths of the day, even to do as Fr. Alexander (of the great *Iliad* question) would say to us at least once a week: "Deny little, Affirm less, and in all cases Make Distinctions!" Such an education will do little to turn our students into what the vocal and committed on every side want us to be—warriors for this cause on the right or fighters for that cause on the left. There is no dearth of extremism, of passionate intensity in this world. If the thoughtfulness cultivated by our arts can put even a small brake on our enthusiasms, or can be a decent refuge from zealotry, well, that *would* be a great virtue.

Unquestionably, there are those in the humanities who pretend to have no idea what we're talking about. "Of course," they might argue, "we make our students more moral! We have taken the liberal arts from being something merely academic, merely antique and intellectual, and brought them into the realm of social justice, into the realm of politics and political activism. Through our teaching, we are producing university graduates who are progressive, supportive of all lifestyles, egalitarian in their views toward income redistribution, critical of narrow patriotism, and cosmopolitan rather than nationalistic in their worldview. Moreover, it follows that encouraging our students to be social justice activists along these political lines is part of the moral obligation of higher education."*

My sense is that many if not most Americans are suspicious, even scornful, of using higher education for political purposes of any stripe. To be thoughtful, to deliberate, and to begin to understand the meaning of personal morality and social justice is one thing; but to preach to our captive audience the answers that we think we know or to be dismissive of common beliefs is another. And moral self-righteousness rarely bears the aspect of virtue. Again, thoughtfulness is a hallmark of the liberal arts; but elitist sanctimony is another reason why much of the public finds itself so alienated from the liberal arts.

In trying to discern the benefits of a good liberal education to us as individuals, what shall we conclude? In the domain of utility, the liberal arts do not bake bread, nor do they mend fractured bones; in the realm of moral virtue, they do not always work to soften a stony heart. But they can keep us from being ruled over by slogans and the untutored opinions of those around us; they can give us greater insight into matters of great importance; and, in a most practical way, they give us insight into our character and the character of those we meet. I still think, as I said in the introduction, that it's better for most of us to see secondhand the baser parts of our nature rather than always to experience it firsthand, up close and personal, from Vinnie the Butcher.

* * *

---

* Note that I did not say that the left-leaning factions of the university encourage "moral relativism," the great moral boogeyman of conservatives. In all that we have seen over the years—the shutdown of classes, the call for greater activism, the chants demanding the elimination of courses in Western civilization—where was there ever any hint of moral relativism? There are a dozen ways to describe these positions—from evidencing a sincere passion for justice to fanatical radicalism—but relativism? I don't think so.

Now let me turn this analysis away from how a liberal education might benefit us as individuals and consider what I'd most like us to see—how a liberal education is of value to our country.

Let me return to what I know best, the American founding. I believe that if you told any of the Founders that the highest knowledge is knowledge for its own sake, or knowledge untethered from any practical use, or learning only for our own edification and delight, or even learning for our own personal liberation, they would have found it hard to agree. Once again, consider Jefferson. Jefferson was perhaps the most liberally educated person of his day. It seems likely that he could read in six languages and was fluent in four. There was hardly a scientific teaching up to his time of which he didn't have knowledge; nor were there many classic or philosophic texts beyond his understanding. After the Library of Congress was burned during the War of 1812, his personal library (all 6,487 books) became the basis of the new congressional library.

Linguist. Scientist. Philosopher. Yes, all of that, but more than that. His education also made him an amateur archeologist, a skilled architect, a valuable diplomat, our third president, founder of the University of Virginia, and the eloquent author of those basic principles of liberty and equality that gave America hope and direction. Jefferson learned from the study of modern political philosophy the self-evident truths that lay behind the writing of his, and our, Declaration of Independence. Spurn its history or disdain its author, but know that without it and the vision of human equality which the Declaration contains, we would not be this country.

Or consider Lincoln. If all his education did was make Lincoln into a private man useful to himself in his everyday life, few of us would notice, and none of us would truly care. What we should appreciate about Lincoln—and before him all the great men of the founding of our country—is the awareness that what was good for them as private intellects might also be of great value, of great use, to creating and then recreating a whole nation, perhaps a whole world.

Or consider James Madison. Without his study of the troubled history of all prior democracies or his inquiries into all confederacies, both classical and modern, coupled with his deep reflection on what we were once bold to call "human nature," Madison could not have become the Father of the Constitution. Without their philosophical, political, and historical studies of the preconditions of popular governments and the nature of tyrannical rule, Madison, Hamilton, and Jay could not have written *The Federalist Papers*, nor could the populace have read and understood them. It was hardly modern political science that was behind the making of America—it was the liberal arts.

Or think of John Witherspoon, a professor of moral philosophy and early president of what would later become Princeton University. In ways far from modern commencement addresses, Witherspoon famously admonished his students: "Do not live useless and die contemptible." To Witherspoon, to go to college and not draw from it things—many things—of use to oneself and to the world at large would have seemed a tragic waste. Recognizing that among those who went to Princeton and listened to President Witherspoon were nine future cabinet members, twelve governors, twenty-one senators, thirty-nine congressmen, three Supreme Court justices, a vice president, and a president (James Madison) who was also one of five of Witherspoon's students at the Constitutional Convention, I can only assume that Witherspoon thought it was particularly contemptible to be useless in the public realm, not just ineffectual in our private lives.

Even in saying all this we have not gone far enough.

Yes, the liberal arts were able to help raise up statesmen for this country when it was most in need—at the beginning and again when we were on the brink of the great dissolve. But let us remember things more ordinary: Few of us are called to be great leaders in this or that aspect of high public life. We are called to be parents, friends, neighbors, and citizens.

The study of Western civilization, its history and works and thought, was absolutely needed in our early leaders and rulers, but what of today? We live under a democratic government whose rulers are not appointed or anointed but whom we choose. Yes, the liberal arts may have once been the domain of aristocrats and gentlemen rulers; but in this democracy we are all rulers. So what characteristics should we want our co-rulers to have? To be ignorant of the past? Ignorant of our laws and mores and the reasons behind them? Forgetful of those who sacrificed to uphold them? Do we look for neighbors who are crude, blind to the beautiful, devoted to their own daily tasks and little else? Who in the world would want to be ruled by people like that?

The list goes on. Should we, as a people, be unaware of our history or the history of other countries? Should we live in ignorance of our national principles and the arguments for them? Should we know ever so little about the roots, attractions, and limits of other principles, principles perhaps antagonistic to our own? Should we be manipulated by the latest slogan or the newest emotional crusade to come along? Should we be swayed by demagogues or by appeals to our passions and our biases? Should we choose as our leaders "celebrities"—those whose only claim is for being known for being known? Have we not suffered enough living under those who lead knowing ever so little, adulated by and drawing their strength from the "poorly educated"?

Is not the answer to all these questions evident?

* * *

Madison writes in the Tenth Federalist that there were three evils—he called them "diseases"—to which all democracies historically are prone: ignorance, instability, and injustice. The last two could, he hoped, be mitigated by constitutional arrangements and institutional structures—the separation of powers, checks and balances, federalism, and the like. But no political arrangements could solve the first problem, ignorance. For that, a rich, broad, and liberal education would be the foremost remedy. And not only for our leaders but, just as important, for all of us who choose our leaders. As Madison wrote, "What spectacle can be more edifying or more seasonable, than that of Liberty & Learning, each leaning on the other for their mutual & surest support?"* You may rest assured that Madison did not think that what passes for liberal education today would be enough to sustain this country and our democracy.

* * *

As we near the end, perhaps I should return to Newman. He put his emphasis less on the political and more on the social.

---

* From James Madison to William T. Barry, August 4, 1822, Founders Online, National Archives, https://founders.archives.gov/documents/ Madison/04-02-02-0480. Even though he was the "Father of the Constitution," Madison knew that what he created was not enough to support our democracy without help: "A popular Government, without popular information, or the means of acquiring it, is but a prologue to a Farce or a Tragedy; or perhaps both. Knowledge will for ever govern ignorance: And a people who mean to be their own Governors, must arm themselves with the power which knowledge gives."

Our studies aim, he wrote, "at raising the intellectual tone of society, cultivating the public mind, supplying true principles to popular enthusiasms and fixed aim to popular aspirations, giving enlargement and sobriety to the ideas of the age, and refining the intercourse of private life." *

Consider the intrinsic civic importance of each and all of these tasks, tasks of refining, raising, enlarging, and cultivating. Together they form a kind of communal sensibility and solid, deep civility. If a barbarian is a person on whom no argument makes an impression, then one fruit of the liberal arts is to de-barbarize civil life and give it some notions of rationality and beauty. Far from non-utilitarian and merely private, the liberal arts are starting to take on the color of necessary, highly useful, and civic.

If the liberal arts can contribute to many of the things we have discussed in this chapter—if they can preserve for each new generation of students the works and lives of the greatest authors, thinkers, and statesman of the past; if they can make the next generation of Americans smarter about things that truly matter; and if in refining the tone of society, they might make our lives together more civil and civilized—then perhaps I do believe, contrary to Mr. Buckley, that such an education should at least be *offered* to each and every American.

One last thought, this time on justice. As unfashionable as it is in some circles to say, the liberal arts once gave a lovely gift to society: It transmitted the great heights of culture, *this* culture, to everyone. While other parts of a university education might be progressive and forward-looking, a decent liberal education had no hesitation in looking backward. It understood it had a liberating aspect as well as a *conserving* function to play.

---

* Newman, *Idea*, 191.

It preserved for everyone (not just the elites) beautiful music, fine art, high culture, fabulous literature, great poetry. In this regard, it wasn't ashamed to be Western, or even what the self-righteous call "Eurocentric." Indeed, it had a kind of honest pride in being the caretakers of such wonderful treasures, *our* treasures. Liberal education once knew that keeping the culture alive was one of the most publicly *useful* things it could do. It gave beauty and intelligence, tone and cultivation, as Newman says, to the whole society.

In this way, the liberal arts were for more than the enjoyment of a few lucky students or only the domain of the rich and well-born—they were a gift to everyone. Back then, critics did not dismiss Dante and Homer as dead white males; neither did readers, the children of working men and the grandchildren of immigrant women, disparage them. In fact, in the past humanists actually thought, rightly so, that keeping Shakespeare alive was a universal gift, not an act of ethnocentrism.

Having been given such treasures, it is now our turn to repay Shakespeare and Milton, Aristotle and Madison. So we repay them as only we can—by keeping them alive. Their bodies, as I said before, may be dead, but *they* aren't. And keeping the words and thoughts and works of great men and women alive is not only of the highest use for us individually and as a society but an act of repayment, of *justice*, to each of them.

{ 17 }

Finally, Where Do We Go from Here?

We've covered much in this small book.

We started by urging the liberal arts not to be so haughty when it comes to other forms of education. In so many ways, there is much that we might appreciate in and learn from them.

We then looked at what might be causing our ever-so-evident decline: not simply the attraction of jobs and money more easily promised by professional or vocational studies but, most especially, the many self-inflicted wounds suffered by the liberal arts over the years. Yes, these include the narrowness of our scholarship and the rise of specialization, the smallness of our vision, the misunderstanding of multiculturalism and all that followed in its wake, the rise of an identity politics that divides rather than unifies our classes, and the undermining of the great tradition of Western learning by contemporary politics and smug ideology.

We then, after a few small but interesting excursions, returned to the theme of the book and asked what could possibly be said about the worth, the value, even the *uses*, of a liberal arts education.

We began with the knowledge, first, that there is no over-abundance of intelligence in this world and, second, that you cannot be an agent in the civilizing of young men and women while jettisoning the best works of civilization.

We began with the knowledge that liberal education has little chance of liberating our students' minds if it is seen as a handy tool for propagating today's political and social opinions, no matter how fine-sounding or high-minded those opinions may appear.

We began with the knowledge that it is hardly elitist or reactionary to preserve the best that has been thought, written, and said in nearly three millennia and offer that to our students, students of all classes and every background.

Perhaps most centrally, we tried to show not only how a solid liberal arts education is of immeasurable value to each student but, above that, how it is of value to our culture and our country.

Reforming the Curriculum

If this book is even partly right that the undermining, the jettisoning, of the traditional liberal arts curriculum lies close to the center of our problems, then reforming and restoring some variation of that curriculum is both the necessary task and, sadly, in many cases, the most difficult.

But to say it is difficult "in many cases" means that in some cases, the possibility of real reform remains. If our situation were not, at least in part, reversible there would be no reason to go any further. But I think it is reversible—no, not everywhere, perhaps not even in a majority of colleges and universities. I'm conservative enough to understand that, in this world, good things often fail, and all living things ultimately die. But there are enough examples in our literature of a remnant returning, of stones that were rejected becoming the new cornerstones, and of resurrection and glorification, not just of death and destruction.

So let us lay out a few simple principles and after that see what we might build.

Perhaps the place to start is to recognize that a student is not really liberally educated if all he or she does is take a few random courses in three or four liberal arts fields—say a course on local criminal justice systems in political science, then maybe a course on the literature of some place or time in the English department, then a course in psychology or film criticism—and majors in some field or another. Not that each of those courses might not be excellent—but they don't *add up* to anything. The liberal arts aren't about picking and choosing. They're about a wide-ranging program of studies that covers broad topics and important human questions in rich fields. And a grab bag of specialized courses picked out of a distribution system that contains a hundred other courses isn't a liberal system no matter what our universities might try to say.

What else should we keep in mind from the start? Well, students, when choices are given, please try to discern what's core from what's marginal. A newly minted professor may be a superb and energetic teacher, but be wary of narrowness.* The injection of graduate school analyses and specialization

---

* Be especially careful of what looks like someone teaching his dissertation. We all know how common this can be and how hard it is for the faculty to police this kind of activity with their new hires. I once abandoned a class I really wanted to take on Chinese history, about which I knew far too little, when, after three weeks, the instructor was still trying to explain exactly how the peasants could send memorials to the emperor. Or when a newly hired biologist at a small inland liberal arts college that I was asked to help thought it would be good to have his first-year science classes begin with a careful study of the sex life of marine worms. (See "A Message to High School Teachers and Principals" near the end of this book.) What might make for an important doctoral thesis rarely translates well into a basic liberal arts course.

into the undergraduate curriculum has done much to diminish liberal education. Gone today in too many places are the stories that showed us the world with its joys and sorrows, gone all our marveling over the varieties of human types or tales of honor and treachery, of hopes ascendant and hopes dashed. Yes, specialization has been the engine of progress in many of the advanced sciences and technology, but it is also the cause of so much smallness of both mind and vision in the humanities.

Above all, be wary of courses that hope to convert rather than instruct. The existence of manipulative education and political correctness are often denied by those in the academy— even when they are ever so obvious to even the most casual outside observer.

So how do we make the nearly impossible possible? First, we need to recognize that left to their own devices, things will get worse. It will take leadership—leadership from presidents, provosts, and deans; leadership from those parts of the university that have an interest in the reform and promotion of traditional liberal education; leadership from alumni and trustees; and leadership from donors.

Let's start with money. When it costs just as much for a student in English—who wishes to read great literature in a seminar with an instructor and other like-minded students—as the university charges its engineering majors or those in premed or business, the liberal arts are mortally wounded. We all recognize that, by and large, liberal arts graduates will struggle financially more than those in more lucrative fields. Yet they are effectively called to subsidize the education of budding petroleum engineers and computer scientists. You can quibble with this all you want, but to ask liberal arts majors to pay even close to what those in more remunerative fields pay is to beggar the poor to support the future wealthy. And, since students may be uneducated but not dumb, it also beggars the enrollment and health of the liberal arts.

Yes, I know, universities look to attract students with their finest facilities, residential quarters, and sports teams, and such things cost real money. And I know all too well that all universities are under legal and regulatory compulsion to have myriad deans, directors, and counselors for scores of things not directly related to instruction yet which cover all students regardless of their course of studies. But we also know that there are colleges that have managed to moderate these expenses and keep tuition within reason. It depends, of course, on leadership.

And, truly, it also depends on money. Donors, both alumni and philanthropic, who have an interest in the restoration of traditional liberal arts curricula, can direct their giving to exactly that cause. Consider, for example, Assumption University in Massachusetts. Here one generous family established the D'Amour College of Liberal Arts and Sciences. which contains not only a good core curriculum but offers a superb minor, "Core Texts and Enduring Questions."

Or consider the Jack Miller Center, on whose board I serve. Over the years, the JMC has built a community of professors and teachers dedicated to teaching American history, principles of democratic government, and constitutional law and history. Through the generosity of the Miller family and others, the JMC has been able to offer fellowships and grants, run a number of higher education programs, support a scholarly journal, and continue its work with teachers of history in high schools.

And, beyond money, the reform and regeneration of liberal education can sometimes find friends in unforeseen places. Traditional liberal education may not have many allies in the now more politically "woke" departments that have steadily increased in number within the liberal arts. But it does have allies in many programs elsewhere—in business, law, medicine, and the sciences in graduate schools. They often appreciate what we have and can do in raising up thoughtful, careful, and knowledgeable undergraduates, many of whom in the past came better prepared for professional school than others. If you need help convincing those in charge of undergraduate liberal arts restoration, try enlisting the deans and faculty of professional schools to the cause.

Nor are undergraduate programs in more technical and professional areas always antagonistic to traditional liberal arts education. Indeed, almost all universities once had a serious core program that was the foundation of the rest of a student's collegiate career, a core from which students would then choose a major in history or computer technology, English or finance.

Let me give an example from what I imagine might seem like a most unusual place: Iraq. Iraqi higher education was no stranger to technical courses; no totalitarian country is. Despotic regimes need engineers and doctors and architects as much as any other. But what they don't need, as you might guess, are the liberal arts. Young people studying history, politics, comparative religion, and philosophy? Students looking into democratic theory or the philosophy of liberty? Or students, as we mentioned in this book's early pages, reading Thucydides and asking questions about international relations, religion, democracy, autocracy, and the causes of war? What could be more subversive to any form of totalitarianism than the liberation of the mind? Jefferson said that democracy and education went hand in hand, not tyranny and free inquiry.

So it's a matter of real interest when a new university dedicated to liberal as well as professional education can get itself started in so remarkable a place as Iraq. But that's exactly what happened just over a decade ago. Starting with just 45 students in 2007 (there are now over 1,600), the American University of Iraq in Sulaimani (AUIS), in the Iraqi Kurdish area, is a comprehensive liberal arts university, offering an education where the liberal arts live and thrive along with various professional and technical courses.

All AUIS students take a four-course Civilization sequence, studying developments in politics, culture, science, and the arts from antiquity to the present. All students also take three math courses (usually college algebra, statistics, and precalculus) and three English courses. The final set of mandatory courses all students at AUIS take is life sciences and physical sciences and one course in computer science. In addition to these thirteen required courses, students are required to take one elective course in each of the three major fields—social sciences, humanities, and math and natural sciences. (Recently, the university celebrated Shakespeare Week in commemoration of the 450th anniversary of his birth, followed in 2014–15 with a week commemorating Galileo's birth—including stargazing using student-made Galileoscopes, several academic presentations, microscope building, and a performance of scenes from Bertolt Brecht's *Life of Galileo*. All of this is serious learning; none of this is fluff.)

Looking beyond its curriculum, Iraq used to be a place where not only were the subjects narrow and specialized, but the mode of learning was as draconian as Saddam Hussein's politics: Lecture…Memorize…Repeat; Lecture…Memorize…Repeat. If you wrote down everything the professor said, exactly as he said it, and repeated it back on the exam again exactly as he said it, you got a good grade. If you didn't get it exactly right, not such a good grade followed. No thought, no questions, no imagination allowed. Even raising your hand in class was discouraged. The textbook and the professor were the experts;

the best you could hope for was to succeed by learning what they said exactly as they presented the material. But the liberal arts are more than content, more than subjects. They are indeed "arts," skills—and skills learned best in the give-and-take of conversation and collaborative inquiry. (One can just imagine what Saddam might have thought of that!) Again, both the content of instruction and the mode of instruction work together toward the liberation of mind and imagination at AUIS.

These are students who now have a small sense of what it really means to be free—to see the world and see it in its complexity and wonder, to explore and read and think for oneself, and to make of one's life what one can through reading, deliberation, and choice.*

Liberal education may be having a hard time of it in America these days. But sometimes it's true that the stones that the builders reject do wind up becoming the cornerstones in other places, amazing places.

What else can be done? Sad to say, there are any number of reasons—the latest pandemic not the least of them—that more than a few small, perhaps residential, private liberal arts colleges may close their doors. A group of alumni, spearheaded by a wealthy donor or two and aided by some of the organizations dedicated to liberal education, could possibly restore life to such places—or begin new ones. I have no illusions regarding how much money it will take—yes, millions on millions. But if there's a will and the resources to do it, it will happen.

As to the idea of beginning new universities, the fanfare surrounding the newly proposed University of Austin (UATX) has been remarkable. Spurred on by the erosion of liberal arts instruction at so many of our finest colleges and horrified by

---

* See Thomas Friedman, "Iraq's Best Hope," *New York Times*, June 4, 2014, A23.

the politicization of university education and the silencing of heterodox opinions of every stripe, some of America's most noted professors, journalists, university presidents, public intellectuals, and philanthropists have laid the foundation for a new and seemingly controversial university. So long as they can break away from the breathless media hype of UATX being primarily an anti-"cancel" institution of clashing opinions and regain some notion of a university as a place of reasoned discourse and wide learning, it should become a model for much of higher education. *

One last word on resources: When I was president of St. John's, we clearly couldn't raise money by relying on our non-existent sports teams. But we could get outside help by doing what we did best—teaching the great books—and doing it for adult, out-of-school audiences. We said before that as liberal arts education has declined in academia, other forms of instruction have arisen to take their place: online Great Books and Great Courses offerings, Garrison Keillor's *The Writer's Almanac*, serious book clubs, and the like. † St. John's College in Santa Fe has two programs we started when I was president there: One is called Summer Classics, where ordinary citizens come to take small, intensive seminars reading great books. Perhaps Plutarch, or Milton, or selections from Tocqueville. We also began offering a number of Executive Seminars for ten to twelve businessmen and other professionals who are willing to

---

* Please see appendix D, "Freedom and Truth in Higher Education."
† Soon after Stanford abandoned its CIV course I was asked by the New School for Social Research in New York to re-create two semesters of that program for interested adults in the city. The program began with perhaps thirty-five attendees and, by the time it finished, I believe we had close to one hundred or more. It was this project that became the foundation for the Summer Classics program in Santa Fe, which draws participants by the hundreds each summer. All this because of a felt hunger for serious education on the part of ordinary men and women in great books and the humanities.

spend a week's vacation time going to exceptional places (say, Rome) and studying with some of the finest of our instructors an appropriate text or texts (say, Shakespeare's Roman plays). These two programs are examples of liberal education at its finest, and they raise up devoted supporters of liberal education.*

Finally, although I've written this book to help my colleagues, students, and the general public better understand what's afoot in today's colleges, I want you, dear reader, to pay some attention to the essay entitled "A Message to High School Teachers and Principals" that appears in this book.† This letter may read like the last word on the matter, a summary of all the chapters in this book. But the truth is opposite: These pages were the *start* of this book, and I wrote them with high school teachers in mind. I'm leaving it as I wrote it since I think it remains important in itself as well as a pretty good distillation of the whole.

∗ ∗ ∗

I had a good idea what I was facing in writing this book. Education is forever a topic of some strongly held views and deep emotions. There are those on both the right and the left who think invective is more effective than argument. And, far too often, they are correct. We all know that reason often loses to passion; it's a problem as old as Socrates. Paradoxically, it was this exact problem that liberal education, in greatest measure, hoped to mitigate: To think, to reason, to weigh arguments, to see alternatives. Not to live a life of mere opinion, but to understand, as best we can, the truth about the most important

---

* See the last few pages of "The Politics of Reading" (appendix F), for a compact explanation of how we might approach teaching and reading great books, especially for such audiences.

† This essay has a companion piece entitled "A Message to High School Seniors" included in the back matter.

human and natural things. And to overlay on that stupendous task some appreciation of the imaginative, the joyful, the beautiful—even the comic.

Moreover, we also know that the liberal arts were never rock solid in a nation such as ours, a nation that prizes utility, progress, and production. Here our studies always had an air not only of the antique and backward-looking but also of the ineffectual and even pointless. And, in a nation dedicated to liberty, equality, and democracy, the liberal arts always seemed to have about them the additional remnants of aristocracy and elitism. What this means is that, in our context, in our contemporary American context, any defense of the liberal arts must show that it is more than a museum of past ideas and events, and definitely more than merely a smug and academic critic of the passing scene. It has to show itself of use, of value, of worth, to the most practical, most progressive, most forward-looking and motion-filled, most modern, diverse, and democratic culture ever seen in world history.

So I wanted to tie the liberal arts back to its role in the health of the country. My guess is that, for the liberal arts to live and again prosper, we will have to show that there can actually be an *American* liberal education—one that helps civilize all of us by preserving the finest in our culture's literature, art, music, and philosophy and that offers them all students; one that encourages all students to understand the basic principles of science and its marvels so that they can be intelligent citizens in our highly scientific and technological world; one that does not see itself as educationally separate from our colleagues in business, law, agriculture, engineering, and other technical and productive studies but that offers what it truly knows and which, in turn, looks to be open to education from them; one that helps this country understand itself and the principles that undergird it; one that has regard for the qualities of our fellow citizens and has the desire to improve their lot and not merely criticize it; and perhaps above all one that makes us smarter in areas that really matter. That is, an American liberal education that satisfies the Founders' hopes that this nation's citizens would be so knowledgeable about history, so cognizant of their duties, so intelligent about the alternatives, and so thoughtful regarding the principles that give life to the country, that indeed, as Madison said, liberty and learning would continue their high task of giving faithful support each to the other.

APPENDIX A

Lincoln, Statesmanship, and the Humanities

It is something of an embarrassment—it may almost be scandalous—for educators in the humanities to write about the education of Abraham Lincoln. Lincoln—lawyer, inventor, philosopher, writer, and statesman—had, by his calculation, less than a year of formal schooling all totaled. He went to school, as he said, "by littles." He never set foot in a classroom after he was fifteen, and never, it would seem, did he speak of his former teachers. When elected to the House of Representatives in 1848 he had to fill in a standard government form (they had standard government forms even then) and in the blank after "education" he wrote "defective." So it is not without its humbling irony for American educators to reflect on the training and career of Abraham Lincoln.

Yet, perhaps, we are safe. For even if Lincoln was not "taught" he was, by any measure, "educated." To those who have a historical interest in the humanities, both Lincoln and his boisterous Illinois audiences can indicate the degree to which

John Agresto, "Lincoln, Statesmanship, and the Humanities," in *The Humanist as Citizen—Essays on the Uses of the Humanities*, edited by John Agresto and Peter Riesenberg (Chapel Hill, NC: National Humanities Center and the University of North Carolina Press, 1981), 57–63.

even the ranks of the formally unschooled were molded by exposure to those areas we now broadly call the "humanities." In Lincoln we can catch a still picture of the scope and breadth of humane learning in the motion-filled life of mid-nineteenth-century America.

But, although interesting, this historic aspect of the humanities in America is only part of the story. In searching for the role of the humanities in America we need to see more than their history. We need to know what good the humanities did and can do. Here again, we can return to Lincoln, not for an insight into what was current in his day but for an indication of the strength, the vision, and the human greatness possible in a mind and a person civilized, that is, humanely educated. If Lincoln shames us by never having been taught, he raises up our profession by being himself a teacher.

Of Lincoln's literary self-education everybody knows a little. We all know that he read the Bible and Shakespeare, although, contrary to our casual expectations, he scanned the Bible for poetic images and studied Shakespeare for the lasting truths of human life. Like others of his generation, he read *Pilgrim's Progress*, *Robinson Crusoe*, Byron, Poe, and Robert Burns. Once, when asked for an account of his early life, he gave his audience not private history but a public literary picture: he quoted to them from memory some words from Gray's *Elegy*. In there, he said, was *his* life, "and that's all you or anyone else can make of it." Unlike his college-trained contemporaries, he knew no Greek and read no Latin classics. At best all he had of the literature of antiquity was a volume of Aesop's fables. But what he did read, he read deeply, slowly, and purposefully.

Shortly before Lincoln was born, another president-statesman,

John Adams, issued a rather fatuous critique of literature and poetry by noting that, amid the bowers of knowledge, philosophers searched for the fruits, the truth, while poets saw only the flowers. Lincoln flatly rejected such hollow caricature. Although Shakespeare and the poets both embellished and strengthened Lincoln's future powers as a writer, his first notion of literature was that it could enlighten and inform, not merely prettify. For Lincoln there was, in literature, the potential to find both truth and flowers. And he attached himself to literature, especially to poetry, because he knew that it was "relevant"—relevant not in any narrow, practical sense, as means toward ends preset by prejudice, calculation, or predisposition, but relevant in the sense that he wanted from literature, as Lord Charnwood, his greatest biographer, said of him, to find in it patterns of what a man's life should be like. He spent no time with all the scholarly crossword puzzles we academicians construct for ourselves in our literary pursuits—influence tracing, historicist reductionism, symbolic reconstructions, or superficial psychological rationalizations. Unlike some of his more educated contemporaries, he studied literature not to learn about it but from it.

Perhaps if we insist on tracing literary "influences" on Lincoln's life and thought we can begin and end with Shakespeare. In the deepest senses of the word, that poet informed him. Especially through the study of the more "political" plays, his mind was given shape and content. We know he read *Lear*, *Hamlet*, *Richard the Third*, *Henry the Eighth*, and *Macbeth*. He sometimes repeated speeches from *Richard the Second*. And upon hearing the news of Lee's surrender at Appomattox, Lincoln gathered his friends around him and read to them from *Macbeth*. His biographers say that he paused at one point and read the following lines twice:

Treason has done his worst: Nor steel, nor poison
Malice domestic, foreign levy, nothing
Can touch him further.

If a Te Deum would be sung for the defeat of Lee and of rebellion it would be in the words of a tragedy of treasonous but
still great men brought down.

Literature not only clarified Lincoln's ideas but strengthened his own capacities as a writer. One of the best examples
of the power and the clarity of Lincoln's own speech is
what he said from the back of his train as it started to leave
Springfield, Illinois, for his first inauguration. This is the
entire speech:

> My friends, no one not in my situation can appreciate my
> feeling of sadness at this parting. To this place, and the kind-
> ness of these people, I owe everything. Here I have lived a
> quarter of a century, and have passed from a young to an old
> man. Here my children have been born, and one is buried. I
> now leave, not knowing when, or whether ever, I may return;
> with a task before me greater than that which rested upon
> Washington. Without the assistance of that Divine Being, who
> ever attended him, I cannot succeed. With that assistance I
> cannot fail. Trusting in him, who can go with me and remain
> with you and be everywhere for good, let us confidently hope
> that all will yet be well. To his care commending you, as I
> hope in your prayers you will commend me, I bid you an
> affectionate farewell.

That little speech is a jewel of majesty, imagery, and depth. It
also was, to the best of our knowledge, impromptu.

One last word on the role of literature in Lincoln's life and
Lincoln's age. On 8 November 1863, two speeches were given at

Gettysburg, and their comparison is shocking. Edward Everett, classics scholar, Harvard graduate and professor, editor, congressman, ambassador, and governor, preceded Lincoln and spoke for two hours. His speech was in the classical style, with literary allusions, mythological figures, and long, elegant, and ornate phrases. Lincoln's speech was only fifteen lines. Like Everett's, it was laden with symbolism, the symbolism (in the midst of a graveyard still covered with unburied dead) of birth and life and childhood. In the midst of death it was a poem about a nation once newborn, "conceived in liberty," and dedicated, baptized, in the name of an idea: that all men were created equal. And it was a speech about the resurrection of that country and those people ransomed by the blood of innocent and brave men, a resurrection into "a new birth of freedom." It was symbolic for the sake of insight, and poetic, too, for Lincoln meant to move men. Perhaps the most startling part of the address is the ironic sentence in the center: "The world will little note, nor long remember what we say here." Lincoln knew its irony, as do we; for he knew that the strength of the immaterial word, "the word fitly spoken," is often the most powerful of all our human forces. He has learned from poetry; and now, through it, he sought to teach.

If Lincoln should strike us as an anomaly in literature, he seems a manifest enigma in philosophy. Within the corpus of Lincoln's extant works there is not one reference to Aristotle or Hobbes or Kant or even Locke. He never studied them. Yet there was not, up to that time, nor has there been since, an American mind more morally clear or philosophically compelling. In political philosophy he studied Jefferson in place of Locke and found himself convinced by what he read. In place of Aristotle or Aquinas he studied the Bible. And, after long reflections, he rejected much of it. His self-education in the humanities gave him a mind that taught him to distinguish and accept, criticize and reject; not a mind that sponge-like absorbed learning and catalogued quotes into holding bins for future use. Philosophy made Lincoln not pedantic but wiser. That, again, was the relevance of the humanities.

To help him in analysis and logic he studied Euclid. He started and mastered the first six books of Euclid when he was forty, in 1848, during his first year as a United States congressman. His crystalline speech would now be clearer, his powers to persuade himself and others even sharper.

Almost alone among his contemporaries, Lincoln cut into the very core of the arguments for slavery. There was no bombast, no spurious pomposity. And although there was pity, there was little sentimentality. "If A can prove," he wrote in 1854, "that he may, of right, enslave B, why may not B snatch the same argument, and prove equally, that he may enslave A?" By the end of Lincoln's analysis, slavery is left intellectually speechless. He could, moreover, recast the most abstract concepts and give them graspable, public life. "This," he said, "is the sentiment embodied in the Declaration of Independence"—"that the weights should be lifted from the shoulders of all men and that all should have an equal chance." As Jacques Barzun said of Lincoln, his speeches glow with both depth of thought and transparency of medium.

Lincoln knew, also, something easily forgotten in a world of rapid technological change and massive economic and military force: the power, the regal domination, of ideas. The idea of slavery's evil, for example, or, conversely, the idea of its positive good, would, in the end, rule history. No people who thought slavery wicked could long defend it, justify it, or forever preserve it in their lives; no people who thought it either good or indifferent could long restrict its spread. For Lincoln, the debates were not spoken or the war first waged to eliminate slavery as much as to eliminate the idea of human slavery. The extinction of slavery could wait, but the extinction of the principle of slavery could not.

To change the course of human events involves, then, the ability to change the course of ideas, to change men's minds. In a democratic government "public sentiment," as Lincoln called it, "is everything. With public sentiment nothing can fail; without it nothing can succeed." A nation whose people know their true aims has little need for enlightened statesmen. In the daily meshing and compromising of public and private interest, politicians, not statesmen, are sufficient. And as a politician Lincoln was hardly a success. Before he was elected president he had spent only two years in any elected national office. He was defeated for the United States Senate twice, he was never governor, he served one term in the House, only to have his party fail to nominate him for another. Lincoln succeeded, not as a politician, but as a statesman-president in a nation puzzled about its purpose and unsure of its true principles. It was here, in a nation torn and confused, where the public powers of the humanities, in the person of Lincoln, began their greatest work.

By an inseparable mixture of accident and inexorable destiny, Lincoln became president. The man who had taught himself Shakespeare and Euclid now ruled. It was, in one sense, a philosophic rule. His insights gave us back the reasons for existence. Through him we saw why this nation was "that last, best hope of earth," that last chance, as he said, for "all people of all colors everywhere" to have the burdens lifted from their shoulders. Through his mind we learned why the question was not, Can free democracies be established? but, rather, Can they endure?

But knowing the truth was not enough. We had to act on it. Public opinion, the final sovereign of a democratic people, is sometimes swayed by argument, but it is more often swayed by speech. The mutability of opinion through rhetoric is, on one hand, surely an ever-present danger in democratic life—Caesar's ambition with Antony's tongue can be more destructive than all the arms of foreign powers. But it also means that the ability to move men's hearts through rhetoric, through speech, must not be absent from the man who would be statesman. Great-souled public men must love rhetoric and speech; such powers should never be relegated only into the hands of demagogues or tyrants. And because what is said can infuse public opinion and give it form, in America what statesmen say is often as important as what they do. For that simple reason the Gettysburg Address, the Speech at Independence Hall, and the Second Inaugural are not only profound understandings of the essence of our nation, they are purposefully superb poetry as well.

In this essay, I have tried to touch on only one small portion of a very large field—how the "humanities" informed and nurtured one historic life. That life, if nothing else, might indicate the power of our disciplines, for they shaped not only the mind of one great man, but the destiny of a great nation. From that life we may get a sense of both the private and the public uses of the humanities, a sense not only of their power, but something of their value for each man and for all men and for all future time.

APPENDIX B

Why Latin? Why Greek?

Twain tells us that Huckleberry Finn, that quintessential American, was fascinated with the Biblical story of Moses. But it soon dawned on Huck "that Moses had been dead a considerable long time." With that, Huckleberry informs us, "I didn't care no more about him; because I don't take no stock in dead people." Since making the case for learning "dead" languages is, arguably, harder than making the case for learning about Moses, what in the world can contemporary Americans say in favor of Greek and Latin?

The first answer everyone seems to give is the one that is in the papers each week: the study of ancient languages, especially Latin, is useful in building English vocabulary, thus helping to raise our children's SAT scores. We read it, and we wince. Is this how low the mighty have fallen? Is the real competitor to Cicero no longer Catiline but Stanley Kaplan and the quickie cram course?

Or sometimes we read that the best reason for learning Latin is simply that it is tough—it teaches "rigorous discipline," it "exercises the mind." For what end? Well, so valuable is the rigor of classical learning that I recently heard of a teacher who

John Agresto, "Why Latin? Why Greek?," *Washington Post*, July 22, 1987. The writer is deputy chairman of the National Endowment for the Humanities.

promotes Latin as good mental training for future computer buffs. A kind of warm-up exercise for the real stuff. O tempora! Such narrow and merely utilitarian arguments are perhaps why a majority of Latin students drop the language after only one year. Surely we need to know the value of these ancient studies, but is there nothing good the classics have to offer beyond vocabulary building, pretechnical training and the academic equivalent of Marine boot camp?

So let us begin a defense of the Ancients with the least popular of all contemporary academic reasons: we read the Ancients because they are ours. These languages and their books, their plays, their modes of thought have helped form not only our contemporary speech but our politics, our literature, our history and the shape of our civilization. If we are to know ourselves, we must know our own. Despite glib talk in certain circles that insists our first job is to open our minds to the understanding of other cultures and ways of life, if we fail to know our own civilization—its hopes, its principles, its reasons, and its greatness—we will not be able to make comparisons that are even worth a dime.

These dead languages and the civilization they embrace are ours: they formed us, almost as deeply as have Christianity and the Bible. To give a small example, not too long ago I picked up my copy of *The Federalist Papers* and turned to one of James Madison's attacks on the opponents of the Constitution. In defending the new Republic, Madison mentions, in the space of about two pages, Minos, Theseus, Numa, Tullius Hostilius, Brutus, Servius Tullius, Romulus, Crete, the Locrians, Rome, Athens, Sparta, and the Achaean League. Madison, the Father of the Constitution, was just as much at home in Greek and Latin as he was in English and French. But *The Federalist Papers* were not essays written for a convention of classics professors. They were newspaper articles, read on the street.

In forging this new nation, this Novus Ordo Seclorum (you can read these words in Virgil and on the back of a dollar bill), any number of Americans knew their Athens, their Rome, their Republicanism, and their Latin, and knew them as something living, not dead. The problems of Athenian democracy were not far from our own problems. Socrates's questions about human excellence are still our questions.

Nevertheless, the Ancients are not completely ours. If the thoughts of antiquity mirror our own in all or even most particulars, if we are their direct and exact descendants, then there is less, not more, reason to study them. Or if the progress of the human mind was such that the Romans and Greeks were mental children and we are smarter, more thoughtful adults, then looking back is merely an antiquarian affectation. It is only because Homer and Herodotus and Cicero and Socrates are like us, but not exactly, that they are worthy of attention. Locke, Madison, Marx, and Nietzsche would not have been possible without the civilization and politics that stemmed from Plato and Aristotle. But they are not Plato and Aristotle. Indeed, their conversations with the Ancients are profound debates, arguments that take seriously the alternatives defended by those who lived before modernity. Arthur Miller is not Sophocles. Sophocles has a different insight into human tragedy from the tragedy of Willy Loman. That's why we read Sophocles. In the Ancients we see parts of ourselves more clearly, yet refracted slightly differently. And we see this other side in texts and through languages that move us from within.

Properly taught, the classics inhabit the best of all possible worlds. They can appeal to the desire to know ourselves, to see the roots of our principles, ideas, and culture and, at the same time, to see who we are not. People who speak as the Romans did are not the people we meet every day. The examples of

Achilles, Hector, Odysseus, Priam, Penelope, and Antigone teach thoughts that resonate, yet are still disquieting.

I once met a professor of Latin who taught Roman literature with great misgivings. The Romans kept talking about such unmodern notions as manliness, virtue, the deepest of friendships, nobility, baseness, revenge, honor. It made him uneasy. This unease, not vocabulary building or the chance to play in togas, is the true value of Latin and Greek.

Yes, we can learn "about" the Ancients and become pedantic. We can do our Latin declensions and hope to jump up a notch on the college boards. Or we can try to learn some things from the Ancients, and do it in their languages and with their ears, and become broader, less provincial and more deeply educated. Despite all our contemporary pride, they still might have the best books.

There is one thing more to say, and it has to do not with searching for truth but with beauty. The ancient languages and their poems and plays and dialogues have unrivaled charm, power, and grace. They have the singular ability to help us free ourselves from vulgarity. I do not mean "vulgar" in the Roman sense of "common." The Greeks had a more insightful word for vulgarity. They referred to it as *apeirokalia*, the lack of experience with things that are beautiful. The Parthenon, Euripides, the perfection of each Platonic dialogue, the sound of Greek sentences—all these have the power to raise us up, not simply our vocabulary scores. It hardly qualifies as the most practical argument to make, but as we work over our Latin declensions, difficult as they might be, we might soon get the sense of something precise, something proportioned, something noble, something truly beautiful. Salve.

APPENDIX C

Further Thoughts on Stanford and Diversity

The teaching of the history and works of Western civilization has been mired in controversy for well over thirty years. The dispute has reached as high as the Supreme Court, mined down into the roots of educational theory, and changed the practice of teaching and learning from grade school to doctoral programs. These controversies are not simply educational disputes of interest mostly to professors and graduate students but have taken on the character of pitched political battles.

This pressure for increased "diversity" in education had one of its first and surely its most consequential iteration in the late 1980s, at Stanford, with the very public, very open, and very strident demands that the traditional and "Western" nature of its basic curriculum be changed.*

What took place was that a quasi–Great Books course that stretched across the entire first year, a core requirement for all incoming students, was, in 1988, reduced from fifteen authors or readings to six. The original fifteen selections ranged from the

---

* I tend to put "Western" in quotes since so much of passes for Western (read: European) was not originally so. Think, of course, of the Semitic literature of the Hebrews or the Archaic nature of the *Iliad* and the *Odyssey*. Just one small indication of what we may rightly call the true "multicultural" range of Western civilization.

Hebrew Bible, a New Testament Gospel, Homer, Plato, Augustine, Dante, and Thomas More through Machiavelli, Luther, and Galileo, down to Voltaire, Freud, Darwin, Marx, and Engels. In addition to this there was a "highly recommended" list of another eighteen works by Aristotle, Virgil, Aquinas, Shakespeare, Locke, Rousseau, Mill, Nietzsche, and others. A fairly extensive curriculum—heavy in its religious and philosophical focus, lighter in literature as well the growth of science, and one that fully overlooked America's political and philosophical contributions to the West—but, still, a pretty good introduction to the range of those issues and the scope of the debates that make up the history of Western civilization.

The course's reduction to merely six required authors—namely, selections from the Bible, Plato, St. Augustine, Machiavelli, Rousseau, and Marx—would now be supplemented by works "representative" of other cultures, including works from various minority groups, women, and works that spoke to issues of "class." Indeed, as the university proclaimed in bold letters, all caps: "THE NEW C.I.V. [Cultures, Ideas, and Values] REQUIREMENT INCLUDE[S] WORKS BY WOMEN, MINORITIES, NON-EUROPEAN CULTURES."*

We have been so bombarded by the supposed educational virtues of diversity and multiculturalism that we no longer see how peculiar such a position actually is. Why was it that a program that was meant to be an introduction to Western civilization had to be made into something else? Why was it

* All material in quotes comes directly from the Stanford University News Service, April 4, 1988. Just in case you might have glossed over it, this repeats in virtually every paragraph that "substantial attention to issues of race, gender, and class" will now be "required"; that now works by "women, minorities, and persons of color" are "among the requirements"; and that "issues relating to class, ethnicity, race, religion, gender, and sexual orientation" along with "works by women, minorities, and persons of color" would henceforward receive "substantial attention."

that Stanford, rather than adding courses that might cover other cultures in serious and sympathetic ways, felt compelled to make a survey of the core texts of Western civilization into something that it was not? And why was it that it all culminated in a chant not of "Let's read more minority writers!" but of "Hey, hey, ho, ho, Western Civ has got to go!"

That the study of the pivotal texts of Western civilization is not only the ground of understanding our culture but also the basis for any positive reform was seen as an insufficient argument. Those who fought against "Western Civ" saw it not as central to understanding our culture but only as whiteness, sameness, and hypocrisy. To the reformers, traditional liberal education was not broad, not liberating, not open to diverse ideas, but simply the academic mausoleum of dead white men.

To put it even more strongly, despite all of "the West's" supposed differences, despite all the variety of outlook and habits and political structures it might encompass, the one thing constant in all "the West" is *oppression*. Slavery, the subjugation of women, the exploitation of the poor, tyranny over minorities, homophobia—the history and writings of this civilization, indeed all the religions and philosophies within it, have this in common: the use of power for the oppression of the other. That this may not be particular to this culture but widespread, perhaps even universal, mattered not. Oppression was here, and it needed to be overturned.

✳ ✳ ✳

I've concentrated here on what was subtracted from this one basic Stanford course and in the vocal desire to see it "go." But in its public discourse and public defense, the diversity movement then and now knew how to speak the language of inclusion and integration. For example, every Supreme Court opinion from *Bakke* to *Burwell* that upholds programs of race-based affirmative action repeats the story that diversity is akin to integration, akin to an increased interaction and common conversation.

But reality soon showed itself to be opposite. Rather than the joining of different cultures or a serious comparison of competing outlooks, and despite all hopes of greater comprehensiveness, another aspect of multiculturalism was gaining strength. It was a movement that overtook all talk about inclusion. It was a movement that demanded not the integration of the works of women, or Blacks, or the historically marginalized into the common core but their further separation into separate departments and the further growth of detached "studies." Hence Black studies, women's studies, Chicano studies, and so forth.

These departments and "studies" rarely sought to integrate into or inform traditional courses, and this view of diversity never pushed to invigorate cross-cultural offerings or expand requirements in foreign languages.* In most places, rather, they became instead well-funded separate programs of grievance and outrage.† *If you want to trace the start of political correctness, speech codes, and identity politics in higher education, begin by looking at the rise and then degradation of "multiculturalism" in colleges and universities.*

* * *

---

* Indeed, if the proponents of multiculturalism were really interested in a deeper understanding of other cultures, one would have thought that building up offerings in Chinese, South Asian, or African language studies would have been a priority. But, by and large, you would have been wrong. (How rare was St. John's College in Santa Fe, where I was president, when we included a requirement in either Sanskrit or classical Chinese in our master's program in Eastern classics.)
† I never quite understood the point that many of the opponents of this pseudo-multiculturalism were making by calling it "relativism" or "nihilism." It seems to me hardly that but, rather, an unwavering attachment to particular ideological

A few last words: Multiculturalism and diversity have largely gone from being a means to expand and improve our various course offerings to being ends in themselves. Every aspect of university life—admission, retention, aid programs, the student body, the administration, the faculty itself—now needs to reflect this idea and commitment to diversity. Today, without this commitment *at all levels*, no college or university can be considered respectable or intellectually serious, or so we are told.

Connected to this most thoroughgoing institutional reformation, there's a larger picture of which we should not lose sight: All this ferment has revealed a sea change of *educational* aims and aspirations. Where once colleges talked about excellence as their educational goal, they now speak of diversity. Or think of how the older aims of a liberal education were once touted—namely, exposure to the best that's been thought and written and, through that, some deeper understanding of important matters of universal concern and, through that, personal liberation. Against that, we now repeat the simple demand for "diversity."

There's no way to view this as other than a tragedy.

---

views of the world and a condemnation of alternative points of view. It's not that the works and authors of the West are one way of looking at things and, say, the feminist way another, perhaps just as good. No, to the serious academic multiculturalist, the history and works of the West are insupportable because they are *not* good. Multiculturalism may *look* like cultural relativism on the surface, but it is far from that in fact.

APPENDIX D

Freedom and Truth in Higher Education

This is a tale of college and university administrators (a) who are entangled in an ideology of social justice and diversity that turns them into un-American and anti-intellectual tyrants and (b) who are stupid. Both aspects are worth exposing and no one does it better than Kors and Silverglate. This book is an encyclopedia of administrative asininity and meanness. Finally, having found the rot and described its aspects, they then tell us how to fix it. Sadly, while the diagnosis is pretty much on target, the cure, I believe, is educational hokum, and I wouldn't be inclined to take it.

Let's start with the exposé and diagnosis, the part that is indeed (in the words of the blurbs on the dust jacket) "chilling" and "eye-opening." Although our authors have a rather cynical view of college administrators—as people who don't wish to rock the boat lest their careers be imperiled—the truth is that so many of them are not partisans of self-interest as much as captives of ideology. (I've noticed recently that that

"Freedom and Truth in Higher Education," review of *The Shadow University: The Betrayal of Liberty on America's Campuses* by Alan Charles Kors and Harvey Silverglate (New York: Free Press, 1998), originally published as "Truth v. Liberty: A Confusion of Priorities," *Academic Questions* 12, no. 3 (Summer 1999).

no college president, even the most craven and inane, ends up selling brushes door-to-door. Even those fired for incompetence happily wind up at some college or another, or at some think-tank or foundation.) Sorry to say, the names of highly placed academic administrators who actually do *believe* in the pervasiveness of social oppression, institutional racism, the need for special preferences, and the simple justice of modern multiculturalism are legion. They may not know what a decent program of instruction in the liberal arts might look like, but they firmly believe that it has something to do with celebrating diversity. And it is this ideology that leads to so many of the real horrors related in this book—forcing RA's to wear pink triangles, encouraging separate freshmen orientations based on race, the re-segregation of dormitories, condoning the theft and burning of conservative newspapers, the monitoring of classes to check for professorial lapses into oppressive speech or insensitive phrasings, and the silencing of those who would question, oppose, or ridicule these policies. Speech codes rarely stem from a desire to suppress criticism or simply limit freedom of speech—university administrators might even have in their souls a philosophical or sentimental attachment to the notion of free speech. But they resort to codes as a way of protecting the regime of preference and "diversity" that stands so squarely at the center of what so many administrators think college is all about. *All* the modern collegiate speech codes described by Kors and Silverglate stem from this one, seminal notion: that some groups need protection from insult, ridicule, slights, and (worst of all) questioning.

The first thing to be clear about is that these horrors of injustice and stupidity are, from all I have seen in academic life, not exaggerated. One has only to look at the public contortions university administrators are going through in California and

Washington state in order to continue to judge, weigh, and reward by race for us to imagine their agenda behind ivied walls. Nor, given the compendium of incidents catalogued by our authors, can anyone dare say that the incidents are anecdotal, aberrant, or rare. They happen not willy-nilly but because of widespread practices and policies. They happen at the most prestigious places perhaps even more frequently than at lesser schools. And I doubt if we know more than a small percentage of what's out there. (How many years was Mary Daly forbidding men from taking her classes at Boston College before some students let the fact out of the bag? Eight? Ten?)

What we learn from our authors is the almost unbelievable depth and breadth of the politicization of university life. We learn how, in the service of ideology, even the most innocuous comments are punished with disgraceful severity. We learn that in some places students cannot express views, raise topics, or carry on conversations in the classroom that would be commonplace discussions at their dining room tables at home. Worse, we learn that serious conversations might even be more verboten than offhand remarks. And we're reminded of how often university administrators give in to threats and extortion by the militant leaders of disruptive groups—and how often they justify their behavior as principled and fair.

Institutions that were once dedicated to the examined life are now hotbeds of ideology and indoctrination. Institutions that once changed students' minds by reasoned arguments now change minds by force and punishment. Institutions that once had an educational mission now have a political agenda.

The paradigmatic case of injustice and stupidity is the once that both begins and ends this book—the case of Eden Jacobowitz, or "the water-buffalo incident." The facts are widely known; suffice it to say that Mr. Jacobowitz told a group of late-night rowdies, all black women, to "Shut up, you water buffalo." Because the "victims" were both black and female, charges were brought against Mr. Jacobowitz for violation of Penn's harassment policies. He, to be sure, seemed to have meant no racial or sexual insult—water buffalo, it seems, do not even live in Africa, but in Asia, and, besides, the term, in Hebrew, is a common mild reproach. The administration, for fairly obvious political reasons, pursued the case against both evidence and common sense, and, in general, showed themselves to be both ideologically driven and, well, morons. Worst of all, in my view, they showed their love of injustice by overlooking far, far worse incidents directed against conservatives and white males, proving, once again, why justice is and must indeed be blind to race and gender, and why color and race consciousness in the distribution of rewards and punishments is the moral crime of the twentieth century. (Incidentally, it also proves why injustice has less to do with violations of liberty than of equality, but that's an argument for another day.)

But Kors and Silverglate seem to be of two minds in defending Mr. Jacobowitz. On the one hand they want to stand up for his right to say what he will. ("No law" means *no* law, as we are repeatedly told.) On the other hand, they feel compelled to make excuses for what he said—it wasn't racial, it's a common Hebrew term, he doesn't have a racist bone in his body, and so on. The same seems to be true of others caught in the trap of speech codes; they really are decent folk, done in by the overzealous.

But all this, of course, avoids the issue. Suppose Mr. Jacobowitz had called them "negro (or worse) water-buffalo"? Or "fat, black water-buffalo bitches"? Well, you get the idea. My guess is Kors and Silverglate would defend all of this, too, for they are principled men. But the rest of us might see a different principle than libertarianism at play here. It has something to do with what academic communities are meant to be, something more than nurseries of self-expression.

It would be interesting to review how the ground for the contemporary debasement of inquiry and its replacement by politics—that is, by will and interest—was cultivated from within, by the liberal arts disciplines themselves. It would be highly instructive to review the role that historicism, for example, has had in undermining the notion of truth accessible beyond time and place, or that relativism has had in making us view truth as varied, or individual. Today we are told, on the highest of critical authority, that all arguments are merely rationalizations of power. What was once sought as graspable universally is now seen as neither in our grasp nor as universal. Soon even the words will change: only fools will seek wisdom; the clear-sighted will seek only "wisdoms"—all equal and unordered in value. Given these philosophical underpinnings, it's no wonder that universities no longer seek to clear the path for lux et veritas. Now they're left protecting this group's light and that group's truth. What was once the highest goal of the liberal arts—to substitute knowledge for opinion—is merely a Eurocentric fantasy at best, a power grab at worst. But Kors and Silverglate don't seem to want to look this deep, so this line of inquiry will have to be put off for another time. Still, I mention it because our authors tell us—at least twice, I think—that one man's obscenity is another man's lyric. Such pop relativism might indeed be at the core of their defense of liberty, but I strongly doubt that it's at the core of a worthy academic mission. Perhaps therein lies the problem, not with their catalogue of horribles, but with their cure: Their goal seems to be liberty itself—not as a means of discovery so much as an end. Freedom, not truth, becomes the final goal.

All the incidents, practices, and policies examined in this book are, as Kors and Silverglate say, "betrayals of liberty." But the worst of them are so much more than that—they are betrayals of civilized learning and liberal education. Often, they are attacks on thinking and reasoned discourse, attacks on that true education that can only come from the diversity of arguments and ideas. That someone may be prevented from calling someone else a stupid dyke doesn't bother me. Why, I would even applaud the censorship. What I fear is banning philosophers, theologians, or sociologists from talking about the pros and cons of "lifestyles"—or any significant issue—for fear that some will take offense. The real liberalism of liberal education is the freedom it promises that we will possess our own minds, that we will be free of the shackles of opinion, current wisdom, naïveté, or popular enthusiasms. It has little to do with shouted epithets.

Nor would I accept the argument of the slippery slope. One can forbid obnoxious behavior without threatening academic freedom. In fact, a little civility might even strengthen it now and then. Let me give a trivial example: At St. John's we have the civil tradition of addressing one another in class by honorifics—Mr. Jones, Miss or Ms. Smith. If you insist on Joe or Jane, or worse, you will be asked to leave class. Is this a violation of "free speech"? Well, what else would it be? The government can't force you to speak this way in the streets. But we can and we do. The result? A civility of discourse that seems to lead to better listening, more reasoned responding, more rational conversations. You see, liberty is the *end* of liberal education, not its beginning.

How do we set out to redeem higher education from the political absolutists of either the right or left? Well, not by an ideal that says "enforce current social dogmas" or by an ideology that rests on the assumption that all freedom from restraint leads, as if by some invisible hand, to freedom of the mind. We don't believe this when we establish core curricula or when we have rules regarding requirements in majors, or alcohol policies in the dormitories. Nor should we believe that imposing restraints on obnoxious speech and behavior teaches "censorship [and] self-censorship." Maybe it simply teaches moderation and self-restraint, two virtues *highly* conducive to liberal learning.

Let's be clear on this. The real tragedy of liberal education in today's universities is not that Alan Dershowitz's nephew isn't allowed to show *Deep Throat* during class registration at MIT (more of this anon) but that certain ideas and viewpoints cannot be argued through and examined in class or in conversation. Aristotle on democracy and slavery, Plato on the diversity of opinion but the universality of truth, the Bible on judgement or on the separate role of the sexes, Nietzsche on women, Jefferson on race, Dante on sin...

We have to find a way to allow—encourage—a professor of religion publicly to examine the reasons behind, let's say, the Biblical injunctions against homosexuality without our going to the barricades to defend his right to refer to students in his class as queers and faggots. Toward this end, neither speech codes nor ACLU-type laissez faire prescriptions are commensurate with the problem. What colleges need are administrators who are willing to take a stand in defense of discomforting, politically incorrect ideas in class and conversation without turning our campuses into new versions of Berkeley under the regime of the free-speech, filthy-speech movement of the sixties.

So, where do we wind up? Toward the end of the book do Kors and Silverglate come to the defense of Darwin? St. Paul? Galileo? Spanish grammar? Nope. Instead they defend

Deep Throat. Why? Well, it seems that the MIT Lecture Series Committee tried to eliminate the tradition of showing sexually explicit movies on registration day in Kresge Auditorium. Adam Dershowitz, nephew of Alan, violated the policy. In fact, he did so twice. In the end, of course, MIT gave in to the pressure of this faction, as administrators who lack the courage of their vision always do, and they rescinded the policy. I guess a blow was struck for freedom, yet only those who think that this is the "freedom" meant by liberal education will be happy. Those who think that college means more than this will, once again, be chagrined.

Let me end by changing the focus from the pursuit of the intellectual virtues to the moral virtues. Can one not be against speech codes and the politicization of the university and still be in favor of the moral development of students? Not if one absolutizes "liberty" as the singular excellence of academic life. Not if one says that the request to students "to respect one another's rights and avoid open conflict is in truth a call to self-censorship" (85). "Self-censorship"! That's a strange and useless thing to call moderation, self-restraint, and respect for others. I for one would be loath to give up civilizing, civil-making functions of university life. We do it badly—God knows we do it badly—but we all promise in our literature to try to turn out not only men and women who are smarter, but men and women who are better. Why should our countrymen support us—in either our public or private institutions—if all we do is expand the avenues for personal self-realization without the hope of making decent friends and neighbors, too? Happily for our institutions, the training of men and women in listening, respect, honesty in speech and writing, patience, moderation, and self-restrain—indeed, in "self-censorship"—usually supports rather than detracts from the life of the mind and its development. Happily, we can defend the open-mindedness and freedom of inquiry necessary to learn from Aristotle or Shakespeare or any other politically incorrect thinker without having to support *Deep Throat* or defend the freedom to write "Mary is a whore" on bathroom walls.

In the end what is needed is to find a middle ground between ACLU-style libertarianism—where all is permitted in the name of freedom, and modern-day academic despotism—where the worst is encouraged, in the name of political justice. In the end, what we need and do not yet possess is a reinvigorated defense of what liberal education is all about.

APPENDIX E

On Jefferson

How does looking backward help us to look forward? Let's begin with some humility: We today have no corner on understanding human passions or humanity's deepest questions. We are not the only ones grappling with profound issues of life. So why cut ourselves off from understanding others who tried to grapple with serious and even existential issues and who thought and wrote under the pressure of those very same questions?

If I may, let me again have recourse to the fields of political philosophy and history: I know I've made reference to Jefferson, Madison, and Lincoln before, but I want to look at them again. Two of them were slaveholders, one who helped establish our somewhat "undemocratic" Constitution, and the third was an unschooled man who presided over a ferocious war. Why look backward? Can't we find others who can better talk to us about our issues today?

Well, actually, no.

Concentrate on Thomas Jefferson, perhaps the most controversial of all the statesmen who have shaped our current national life. When Jefferson said that human equality was not only true but "self-evidently" true, what could he possibly have meant? It certainly wasn't true *as an obvious fact*, since there wasn't then, nor is there now, any semblance of perfect equality among people. Jefferson and his compatriots hardly seem unintelligent—they could certainly see what we see, perhaps even with greater clarity. Nor does it even seem true *in theory*, since, if anything, the truth is that each one of us is different, and different in ways that matter. Not just taller or shorter, but unequal in intelligence, in character, in virtue, in everything. "You call this stuff about all men being equal 'political philosophy'?," our critical student might say. "I call it empty rhetoric."

It doesn't seem that Jefferson and his colleagues thought these words, this idea that all men were created equal, to be mere rhetoric. Indeed, they did seem willing to sacrifice their fortunes, honor, and lives on the truth of it. Besides, if the idea is *not* true but rather (as the South said as it began to consider the dissolution of the Union) a "self-evident lie,"* on what do we today rest our belief that egalitarianism is right and just? Is our contemporary belief in human equality also "mere rhetoric"? If equality doesn't stem from a common human nature, does it perhaps stem from custom or agreement or our merely wishing it so? If so, then human equality rests on the shakiest of foundations, since customs, agreements, laws, and ideals can and do change.

If Jefferson and his compatriots believed in the truth of what they said, *what exactly did they mean by it?* They obviously couldn't have meant that we are all the same. They obviously could see that even the most important thing—human excellence—is possessed in different degrees by different people. So what did this thought, this truly *revolutionary* thought, actually entail? Does it mean equality in rights, as the Declaration of Independence seems to indicate later, even if not everyone was enjoying such rights? If so, how can we go from equality to rights, or from equality to liberty, and carry that further to

---

* Sen. John Pettit of Indiana, in the debate over the Kansas and Nebraska Act of 1854.

go from equality to self-government and then an idea of liberal democracy? Is it not clear how a good teacher, by encouraging good conversations and careful, sympathetic inquiry, can deepen our understanding of some of the most important civic issues not only of former times but of ours as well?

But all this is foolishness, you might say. Jefferson owned slaves. And if slavery doesn't contradict the core belief of the Declaration, then nothing does. Again (our student says), it was either mere rhetoric or, worse, hypocrisy.

Hypocrisy? The odd part is that Jefferson, I believe, would agree. He knew slavery was wrong, that it was a moral and social evil. Yet he helped write the Declaration, in which he openly penned his own condemnation. He couldn't do much of anything to change the slaveholding states. At best, he could lay out the principle, as Lincoln later said, that would someday bring slavery to an end. But what about Jefferson himself? He knew with a clarity that outshone many of his contemporaries that slavery was immoral and unjust—that no humans are born, as he wrote, with saddles on their backs and others with boots and spurs, ready to ride them.* He knew slavery displayed "the most unremitting despotism on the one part, and degrading submissions on the other." Knowing this, he trembled, since he knew that God was just.† Yet Jefferson kept slaves throughout his life. To understand this corruption of the heart, or this overriding love of one's self and one's interest, or the possible but deep conflict between fear and self-preservation on one hand and justice on the other, we need to look more deeply

---

* See Jefferson's letter to Roger Chew Weightman, June 24, 1826, Founders Online, National Archives, https://founders.archives.gov/documents/Jefferson/98-01-02-6179. This was the last letter Jefferson ever wrote.
† Thomas Jefferson, *Notes on the State of Virginia* (1781), Query XVIII. For a fuller discussion of Jefferson and slavery see Agresto, *Rediscovering America* (Los Angeles: Asahina and Wallace, 2015), particularly chapter 1.

into human psychology, into moral philosophy, into religious history and its knowledge of the seduction of evil, and into the world's great literature. Working this all out will teach us not only about Jefferson but also so very much about our own thoughts and our country.

Jefferson wrote that all men were created equal, and Jefferson owned slaves. Is there anything worth knowing that we might learn from that? Shall we read Jefferson with even greater care to see why this was so, or will we be content simply to be critical or self-righteous? Shall we start to understand the complex political and even spiritual problem Jefferson forced himself to face when he refused to hide the fact that certain self-evident truths were called into question by his own actions? Or is labeling Jefferson a racist good enough? I cannot imagine students being uninterested in exploring these questions.

APPENDIX F

The Politics of Reading

There was a time when we thought we could just read. We'd pick up a book—say, *Tom Sawyer* or *As You Like It*—and think we were doing something fairly straightforward. Straightforward because, if we were careful readers of reasonable intelligence, we generally thought we understood what we read. Sure, some writers could be obscure or ironic—but often we knew how to adjust ourselves that and still see what was being said. With truly fine authors we could relish the words, enjoy the ebb and flow of sentences, and see the architecture of a piece unfold. We could see the marvel of the human imagination at work. From the very finest authors we could gain not only enjoyment but enlightenment. We no longer had to experience the world in order to know it—we could read and think and grow. A great author could make up our mind or change our mind. We read, we absorbed, and we lived our lives better, deeper, more sensibly—at least so we once thought. Ah, how naïve we were; or so we are now taught.

We once thought that reading was not only straightforward but, contrariwise, magical too—magical, mysterious, and mystical. How else could it be that an author could live

This is a revised and slightly expanded version of a talk given at the Rowfant Club, Cleveland, May 26, 1999, and reprinted, in part, in their Annual Report, 2000. It seems they left out all the parts (here included) which they thought might get them in trouble.

207

on even though dead? How else than mystically, magically, can it be that the one most obvious part of you that lives after death is your mind—so long as you're an author. How marvelous is it that we say the most incredible thing—that we can, through the medium of the written word, "possess someone else's thoughts."

I want to talk about two things—reading as a straightforward activity, and reading as the mysterious transfer of ideas between minds, generally through an object of delight: a book.

Those of you who think of reading as straightforward—you sit down, you pick up a book, you read it through, perhaps you discuss it with friends, and from this you think you might have learned something of what the author has to offer—are probably deceiving yourselves. Or so we are informed.

First, we are told on the best of contemporary academic authority that words are weak purveyors of ideas. We now "deconstruct" texts to find meanings unmeant by the author, meanings the author unwittingly hid behind words. Texts now need to be unpacked to find out what really was driving the author, which inevitably turns out to be a political, social, or economic agenda that our author more likely than not unwittingly served.

But deconstruction is silliness, you say, and no man or woman of sense plays those games with books any longer. It was just a fad. Fair enough, perhaps; but what other games will the academic world play with our authors? Well, how about this—since all authors are creatures of their time and place, captives more or less of their culture, truly to understand a book means to discover the driving force behind that culture, or, to say it differently, to discover the power relations that gave shape to that society. What will one see when he or she peers behind and beneath the pages of an author? Well, of course, either a witting or an unwitting tool of the dominant forces of the society. To read Shakespeare is to learn about the Elizabethan use of women, its fear of blackness, the oppression of the poor, and the victimization of difference.

Why this constant harking back to race, class, and gender? We are told, fairly often and directly, these are the drives, the determinants, the forces that move our social orders and interactions. And these are the forces that drive writing. The work of a true contemporary scholar is to discover, uncover, and expose these aspects of a work, to show the grounds—often, usually, hidden even from the author—upon which all literature is based. And you, straightforward as you are, thought you could just read!

Over the last forty years I've watched all these newfangled political ways of reading sprout up in earnest and, to my way of reading, all seemed fairly beside the point. They made literature small. If this is what great literature is, merely an expression of or cover for the power relationships of a bygone age waiting to be exposed, who could possibly care? If literature can't help rouse me, or delight me, or change my life for the better—if all it can do is show me how unwittingly oppressive life was before our own great age of political insight—why bother?

But that's exactly what modern literary criticism says is naïve, impossible, foolish. You cannot be a straightforward reader, and nothing magical can happen between you and an author. The only proper stance is one of criticism, and not simply literary criticism but what all literature now seems to demand—political, cultural, and social criticism. Your proper role is not to be amazed or grow, to be delighted or even to be changed, but to find out what's really going on. How smug, it seems, we have grown these days in our self-estimation that we are all, now, critics and not learners.

I offer you this as evidence: I decided to pick a well-regarded university and see what it offers in its graduate English program. I chose Georgetown, in part because, when I first thought about this subject, scandal broke in the ranks of its English department. That department had recently dropped Shakespeare as a requirement for undergraduate English majors. They did this partly on the grounds that Shakespeare's view of women was no longer, in their opinion, correct. "We want students to be aware that there are problems in Shakespeare's plays with the way women were portrayed." It seems that even a genius of the male persuasion such as Shakespeare went over the line in thinking he might have something right to say about human relations in general or the female sex in particular.* (Of course, in this age of enforced and celebrated diversity, we wouldn't want to expose students to divergent views, especially views cogently examined and beautifully expressed; but that's the subject of another discussion.) Suffice it to say that undergraduate English majors at Georgetown can graduate without ever reading Shakespeare or, for that matter, very many other first-rate authors.

But maybe, I thought, their *graduate* program would be bet-

---

* The words are those of John Slevin, the chair of the department's curriculum committee. While some multiculturalists were no doubt pleased with this stupendously mindless stand, much of the literate world had a field day with it. Even the hardly conservative-leaning Maureen Dowd could condemn this "rush to multiculturalism" in the pages of the *New York Times*. The English department, "in its dialect of English," could bloviate that henceforward its courses must reflect "the power exerted on our lives by such cultural and performative categories as race, class, gender, sexuality and nationality, and on the ways in which various kinds of representation aid in the construction, reproduction, and subversion of those categories." So long, Shakespeare. Anyone who was deceived by the perjury that multiculturalism and diversity were *adding* to our curricula and not tossing out whole ways of knowing should by then have awakened. Maureen Dowd, "Liberties: A Winter's Tale," *New York Times*, December 28, 1995, p. A17.

ter, more open and open-minded, less politically driven. With that hope, let me share a fairly full selection of Georgetown's English offerings for a graduate degree:*

> This is for students contemplating a Ph.D., for present or prospective teachers of English in secondary schools [!], and for people with already established careers in writing and editing.
>
> *Introduction to Literary Theory.* This course will introduce some of the most important issues in literary theory by studying the history of critical discourse and recent movements in critical thought...We will be concerned with issues like the formation of literary canons, the ideological context of theory, the past and recent institutionalization of theory, and the theory of gender.
>
> *Critical Border Line(ages): One Hundred Years of U.S. Latino/a Criticism.* This course traces a number of critical discursive genealogies, from the work of some major Latin American cultural critics of the late 19th and earlier 20th centuries through the emergence and development of Latino/a critical discourses in the U.S. from the middle of the 20th century to the present.
>
> *Politics of Literary Form.* An attempt to extend, supplement, and revise the formal interpretation of texts through an analysis, at once theoretical and practical, of the political dimension of literary form.
>
> *Cultural Theory and Practice.* An introduction to methods of analysis in cultural studies...Topics of discussion will include structuralism, Marxism, feminism, deconstruction, and film theory.

---

* This list goes on for three pages following. Believe me, I understand if you decide merely to skim it all.

Writing and Revolt in Late Medieval England. This course focuses on the politics of the vernacular in the late Middle Ages, and on the origins of "English" literature in dissent, discord, and subversion.

Constructions of Masculinity. "Lifestages" as charted by third-generation Freudian theorists will provide the focus for comparing texts ...

There *was* a course on Shakespeare in the catalogue: *Contemporary Critical Issues in Shakespeare.* "He was not of an age, but for all time!"

We shall test the truth of Ben Johnson's claim by examining a range of Shakespeare's poems and plays with regard to the political issues and critical methodologies of our own time and place. Cultural materialism, deconstruction, Lacanian psychoanalytic theory and historical phenomenology will provide vantage points for considering scripts that will include some of Shakespeare's acknowledged "masterpieces."

Besides Shakespeare we also have *Dickens*: "A reading of major texts by Charles Dickens in the light of recent critical theory. We will concentrate on the history and theory of Victorian publishing...and gender theory."

How about *Reading Race: Critical Theory from 1500 to the Present*? "We will combine race narratives from the Bible to Shakespeare to contemporary film with critical readings on race from psychoanalytic, post-colonial, feminist and critical legal perspectives." Or another good one: *Whiteness and the American Literary Imagination.*

This course will investigate how selected American writers influenced and were influenced by whiteness...This course will examine the ways in which literature cemented a distinction between white skin—the common pigmentation we associate with those we call white—and whiteness, an invented construct with no genuine content other than a culturally manufactured one...In addition to reading primary texts, we will explore theoretical writings of the nascent discipline, whiteness studies.

Next: *Issues in Cultural Studies.* "We will be analyzing the role of culture as an ensemble of concrete material practices which shape identity through the interlocking categories of race, class, gender and sexuality, among others...The special topic of this year's seminar will be 'Culture and Colonialism: Dominance, Resistance, Reciprocity.'" (I guess this beats taking some boring class in "English" or "literature.")

Feminism and Postcolonial Theory comes next (though I think we may be seeing a pattern developing): "Among the various debates in postcolonial theory, debates on national identity and racial difference have dominated the terrain. By contrast, debates in feminism have focused on the articulation of sexual difference and the construction of gender. This course attempts to forge a dialogue between these two theoretical areas."

Last, my all-time favorite: *History and Theories of Sexuality.* "This course seeks to historicize contemporary theoretical debates about sexuality, in particular gay and lesbian studies and 'queer' theory as it is informed by African-American and/ or feminist theoretical and political concerns. This course is designed as a sophisticated introduction to the history of sex."

Well, enough. Can you imagine taking two or more years of this? Imagine going from this armed with a higher degree, ready to introduce high school students to the pleasures and wonders of literature!*

It's clear to me that contemporary scholars love the use they can make of books, but do they love books? I doubt it. Perhaps that is why the Georgetown English department sees no masterpiece in Shakespeare, only "masterpieces."

Still, the idea of masterpieces—without quotes—may go so strongly against their more sophisticated view of modern egalitarianism that our critics feel *compelled* to expose what they see as the evils, the prejudices, the insensitivity to more modern truths that often lie at the heart of great authors, especially all authors who approach something akin to canonical status. But it's odd: Toni Morrison, Maya Angelou, or Barbara Kingsolver we may heed and read sympathetically; Shakespeare and Milton we will deconstruct and expose.

We are a democracy; we cannot stand a canon. We are egalitarians; we cannot stand to have greatness stand above us.

---

* I have left these examples that were in the original talk. Lest I be accused of peddling out-of-date material, I looked at Georgetown's latest offerings. It seems they no longer offer a PhD but do offer a master's program. Still, I wondered if they might teach Shakespeare. Yes, of course, but in their own way: "Many literary-critical approaches cut their first teeth on Shakespeare—psychoanalytical theory, historicism, feminism, queer theory, critical race studies, post-colonialism, eco-criticism, disability studies—and we will seek out the ways in which these approaches inform the stage and screen." What else might a budding high school English teacher take? How about Disability Studies? "To see how changing conceptions of disability both ground and threaten notions of normality...[topics include] disabled modernism/modernity, disability poetry and poetics; cognitive disability, dependency theory." Then there's both Queer Memoir: Theory and Practice, and Queer Cinema. This last one is a course built around "establishing a zone of inquiry around anti-normative sexual acts" in order to "destabilize" "traditional and restrictive ideas about sexuality and gender." Remember: This is a program meant to help their graduates *teach high school English*! And still we wonder why the humanities are dying?

In the name of politics, we teach far too many of our children and students that the proper doing of literary criticism is the doing of denigration. And what democratic men and women need most—something great and worthy to look up to—is what they now get least. In place of models of human excellence, we get nothing but a wink and a nod; we have now seen through the operation ever so clearly.

This isn't, to be honest, a new story. For example, for the better part of the last unfortunate century we have thought it so much fun to psychoanalyze our authors—not "What is Milton saying?" but "Why does Milton say what he does?" And in asking "why" we are not looking for *reasons* but for *causes*—causes in his upbringing, in his family relations, in his physical condition, in his religious fears. So we try to learn all *about* an author and shrink from learning *from* an author. Indeed, how could we learn from someone who wrote what he did for reasons peculiar and particular to himself? How can there be a transfer of mind when the thoughts were conditioned upon psychological and even physical causes we can never have, for we can never have Milton's upbringing or his psyche?

What I've called here the psychoanalytic view of analyzing books is as destructive of learning as any modern deconstructionism. It not only makes our author mechanical; it distances him from us, makes him other. And no transfer of mind can take place because there were no reasons behind his thoughts, only causes.

Oddly enough, this "analysis through causality" infects *not* the sciences—where one would think causes would be most respected—but the humanities. Ask any scientist why Albert Einstein said that $E=mc^2$ and you'll get an explanation of a set of ideas and relationships regarding time, mass, and energy. We would think a scientist off his rocker if we asked him "Why did

Einstein say $E=mc^2$?" and he gave us causes but not reasons—if, for example, he offered that Einstein was Jewish or that he had trouble with authority, or that Einstein was once thought slow and tried to prove his prowess by later mathematical feats, or that it surely had something to do with Einstein's upbringing. No. We'd not be offered causes by our scientist-expositor but reasons, arguments, real explanations.

But ask a humanist why Martin Luther posted his theses on the church door and you're just as likely to hear that it had something to do with his feelings of inadequacy and subjugation, his relations with his father, or his stomach troubles as with his insights into the nature of grace, sin, and the true church.

In that regard, consider the example of that darling of all high school teachers, "putting things in historical perspective." I know why teachers often do this, and it's generally from the kindest and most generous of motives: Who are we to judge others by our standards? We may be right and they who lived before us benighted; but we should not be judgmental, for they lived in other places, far away and long ago, and had no way of knowing all we know today.

There's a good truth buried in here that needs to be applauded. We should try to understand our authors as they understood themselves. We should let them speak for themselves, and we should listen attentively to their positions. We should not jump to judge them by our standards, not because they had no way of knowing all we know but because our standards may well be wrong or defective and their standards, their ideas, insightful, even correct.

But that's not exactly how the "historical context" school comes across: We forgive our authors their faults because they lived back then and over there. Given their strong minds and fine sensibilities, they would have known more and better except for the accident of time. So everything contrary to our prejudices and contemporary opinions we forgive, and, rather than explain our authors' differing insights and views to our students, we explain them away. We dig up all we can about the "life and times" of someone, then we attach that someone's writing to his or her life and times—and we wonder why our students find our authors so distant, so other, and so uninteresting. After all, we do not and never will live in any past life and time. And our better students understand that so much learning about others truly stands in the way of learning from others.

Worst of all, by placing our authors' views in their "historical context," we keep those views from ever questioning our own prejudices and orthodoxies. If Aristotle wrote what he did because he lived in an aristocratic slave society that put down women, if Dante lived in a society dominated by medieval superstition and overarching church power, and if Lincoln lived in an age saturated with both open and unexamined racism, then how can we expect to learn anything from our authors regarding what moved them most—justice, sin, and the idea of equality?

In the end, if our authors are bound and dominated by their historical context, if they are captives and expositors of their age, if they do not transcend their time and place and are unable to speak to me trans-temporally, trans-historically, then their value to me is diminished—they are, at best, exemplars of their age. But their age, to me, can rarely be anything but a curio. I will never live in ancient Athens or late-medieval Florence or Civil War America. Our greatest and finest authors must in some reasonable way transcend their time and place; otherwise why read them? Really, *why read them*?

Now, less than first-rate authors are probably, to greater and lesser degrees, creatures and exemplars of their horizons, their ages' worldview. But are the greatest minds so bound? I offer you that our finest authors were those who were able to transcend the particular, transcend the politics and culture of their day, and to see some things more universally. Hal as king is stupendous and Iago is despicable not because Shakespeare understood the tenor of his times but because he knew something of the human heart, its heights and its depths, at all times. He knew something of nature, not simply of his time and place. And when *we* are at our best, we are open to having our minds and hearts expanded and filled, even by people who lived in a different historical "context."

I even offer that our greatest authors were not only *not* creatures of their age but often the greatest contrarians their age, often makers of *new* modes and orders. Was Socrates killed, did Locke write in secret, was Spinoza excommunicated—because they exemplified the feelings of the times? I would, to put it mildly, tend to doubt it. And the finest of our authors are those who not only transcend their time but transcend our time as well; they are those who are able to move us to see things with new eyes, to examine our own prejudices and opinions, to gain insight into truth and beauty and friendship when, without them, we *would* be mere creatures of our own time and place.

So, let's stop reading politically, that is, foisting our own prejudices and categories and beliefs on our books, and start reading with the thought that we really might *learn* from the authors of our finest books. Do not assume that change is always progress, that the critic commands the artist, or that smugness and superiority in the face of greatness is an admirable trait in any respectable person.

I want to end by suggesting to you what I like to call Ten Rules for Reading. I wrote these for students of the Great Books, and I acknowledge the fact that they work best with our more philosophical texts rather than our more imaginative and poetic works, but here goes:

1. We will try to understand our author as we think he understood himself. We will try to get into the mind of our author to hear what he is saying to us.

2. We do not care about our author's biography or foibles or parentage or psychoses or socioeconomic status. We care only about his thoughts. We cannot have our author's background or circumstances, but we can have his mind.

3. Learning all *about* an author leads us to pigeonhole, categorize, caricature, and, in the end, dismiss him. Learning *from* an author raises us up to his level. Let us try to meet our authors on their level rather than bring them down to ours.

4. Our authors are not stupid. Let us read each one as if he or she has, for each of us today, the truth, the simple and real truth, about important things.

5. Since none of our authors are stupid, this may mean they are right even when their opinions diverge from our own. This means they might be right even when they hold uncontemporary views on religion, privacy, community, individualism, equality, obligation, education, sex, class, race, lifestyles, liberty, democracy, or any other area where we think truth is now settled.

6. Our authors are not stupid. But they often disagree not only with us and our contemporaries but also with each other. Even though we begin with the assumption that each of our authors can tell us the truth, this can't be true. Some of them are wrong. Sorry.

7. Since our authors are not stupid, they write better than we expect. Don't begin by assuming that they write casually or sloppily or that, every now and then, we'll catch them making silly mistakes. If we think we see a mistake, odds are we're wrong.

8. Our authors do not write about little things. God, man, justice, love, friendship, death, and meaning are not insignificant matters.

9. Ask our authors naïve questions. Like: "Author, what are you trying to tell me? Why do you say that? I don't understand." Great authors love great questions.

10. Begin in humility. Our authors know more and say more than we will ever truly know. But don't be too humble. Our authors wrote for you. They actually think you can learn to possess their minds. Run with them.

A Message to High School Teachers and Principals

I would like to believe that many of the high school teachers and administrators who will read this are the products of a liberal education. If so, at some point your mind was touched by a teacher or your imagination was excited by a field of study. You decided you had a vocation in teaching, so you put aside easier and more lucrative endeavors to show adolescents something of the joys of knowing. Some of you, the best of you, use the classroom, with its conversation and its readings, to expand your own horizons and continue to grow in knowledge yourself. It's been my experience that many of you truly love some aspect of the liberal arts. Even more than many university professors, who can sometimes be devoted more to their research projects than to the broad sweep of their field, you are in love with history or literature or French or science. You persist in this devotion despite all the challenges and disappointments we all know are part of the life of a high school teacher.

Having said that, I hesitate to burden you with another problem, with a thought both true and sad: *If your students do not get a liberal education under your tutelage, they almost certainly will never get one.* And for the great majority, even with the beginnings of a liberal education from you, they will abandon what you love, and they will go on to other things. The liberal arts will not play much of a part in their future lives. To reshuffle some of the figures I set out in the introduction, in one recent year over 300,000 undergraduate degrees were given in business, with only 37,000 in philosophy, English, and history *combined*.

But the problem isn't that so many of your students will go to college with particular career or vocational goals before them. Let's hope that you've widened their interests to a degree that even in the most technical of fields they can find issues and questions that will lead them to continue to expand their minds regarding important human questions. No, my real worries are different. Even if your students do go to an ostensibly liberal arts college, we all know how deeply specialization and "research" have set down their roots, even at that level. I worry that, with your having sown the seeds, they will go to college in search of even greater liberal learning...but the seed will shrivel and die.

Let me give an example. A while back I was a consultant to a small, liberal arts college in the East. It had only about 350 students all totaled, and the science faculty was hoping to hire a biologist. They had a person in mind. He was a recent PhD and wanted to continue to do work and teach his specialty: the sex life of marine worms. I am not, as Dave Barry would say, making this up.

Now the odd part wasn't that he wanted to teach his specialty—that's the wish of ever so many new PhDs—as much as the fact that the college saw nothing wrong with his doing this. Specialization and research-driven teaching is what they themselves as professors knew, and they saw nothing out of the ordinary in this. This or that small topic made up much of their usual regular course offerings. If pressed, they probably would have attempted some defense like "Well, maybe the students will learn a lot about biology by studying a piece of it in depth." How feeble, and how amazingly illiberal, such a view actually is.

We all know it. We know that encouraging a new professor to continue his narrow and specialized research, perhaps turn his dissertation into a book, is hardly an education fit for students who know precious little about biology or even about science in general. For a student to be told that he or she is getting a valuable education through these crabbed means is little less than fraud. And for parents to be told to fork over thousands in tuition money for this stingy and narrow view of education verges on the criminal.

Of course, even at the best liberal arts colleges taking courses in biology, history, or anthropology often means not learning the broad sweep of the discipline but, rather, learning how to be a professional biologist, historian, or anthropologist. I'm sorry to tell you this, but in the vast majority of cases, *the last chance for our children to see the world and see it in its breadth and complexity rests with you. Their last best hope of seeing the broad sweep of this civilization and its works is in your hands.*

This is why I have grown to hate the phrase "preparatory school"—as if you were simply preparers for the real world of learning that follows in college. You are not "preparatory"; you are not the table-setters for the feast that follows. You are often, most often, both the sum and the pinnacle of a student's liberal education. For most of our students the last comprehensive, panoramic, freeing education happens with you.

I want to add two further observations about the liberal arts in our high schools, one bad, one good. First, the bad. I know the degree to which historicism has taken over so much of our collegiate academic analysis. Historicism is part of the reason why much of what goes on in college looks like a defense of cultural relativism. But a kind of pop-historicism has set up shop in our high schools, and while it looks like part of a liberal education, it actually is the antithesis of it.

The code phrase is "looking at things in their historical

context." I know that many of you have used these words, perhaps thinking this is what good teaching and learning does. It certainly sounds benign. And I can imagine a level on which it is benign. If our students read, say, Dante, by all means they should try to understand him as he understood himself and not make him what we would like him to be. Nor does it hurt to know that he lived in the thirteenth and early fourteenth centuries, that he was seriously involved in politics, and that he had a spectacular command of theology, biblical interpretation, and church history. Yet even all this and much of the rest of what we know about him we will learn from reading what he wrote, not reading all we can find in Wikipedia about medieval Florence. (Indeed, much of what we know about his "time and place" we will learn from *him* rather than him from his time and place.) But, still, what the problem?

I worry that by "contextualizing" everything, we don't explain things; *we explain them away*. By contextualizing them, we immediately make them "other." With this, we set up a barrier to learning from the men, women, and events of the past since we do not inhabit their universe. If what Dante wrote and did and thought, he wrote, did, and thought because he was a late-medieval Florentine—if we can only truly understand him by understanding how he was a product of, or reflected, his "time and place"—*then he can teach us very little, since we do not inhabit his world.* Thus, the writers and thinkers of the past become not teachers but curios. Dante becomes a late-medieval religious judgmentalist, persecuted by his political enemies and angry at their treatment of him—rather than a perceptive teacher of, for example, the nature and gradations of good and evil, their motivations, and their consequences.

Now, as I said, this push to contextualize sometimes grows out of the best of motives. Take perhaps my favorite example, Thomas Jefferson. We know that Jefferson wrote that all men are created equal, endowed with inalienable rights that included life, liberty, and the pursuit of happiness. We also know that Jefferson was a keeper of slaves. Knowing this, most every student will pronounce Jefferson a hypocrite. And some teachers will do them one better by saying he was more than that but also a racist, misogynist, and a politician who use fine-sounding words simply as weapons to get his way. Surely he seems a contemptible person all around.

Into this walks a teacher of good will who tries to rehabilitate Jefferson by hoping that if we would only look at Jefferson "in the context of his day and age" we'd not be so hard on him. After all, back then many people, especially well-to-do Southerners, had slaves. Of course Jefferson meant all white men had these rights, not really "all men." It was just a form of words that most anybody back then would use. (And maybe by all "men" he really was saying all "males," since, back then, most men thought women their inferior in many ways.) So there, he's not really a fraud at all, just a creature of his time and place!

Now, look at what we've done. We haven't truly explained Jefferson; we've pretty much explained him away. He wasn't a bad person; he simply was pretty much like everybody else in those times. Besides, we shouldn't try to hold him to our modern ideas of justice and human equality—after all, he lived back then before they knew all that we know today! And so we think we've rehabilitated Jefferson, and we congratulate ourselves on how far we've come in understanding and righteousness all at the same time! (To think, we laugh at the ancient world because we think they made *their* world the center of the universe.)

The trouble is, we haven't really learned anything. We haven't really tried to understand Jefferson as he understood himself; all we did was make excuses for him. And they're probably not excuses he'd accept. Indeed, he might agree with our student that he was, in one way, a hypocrite: for it seems that he most assuredly *did* believe that all men were created equal—one has only to read what he tried to keep in the Declaration about the moral evil of the slave trade—and he *did* own slaves. In either condemning Jefferson (as in the first example) or in excusing him (as in the second), all that our students might have learned from Jefferson's dilemma about politics and human nature is withheld from them—about the attempt to make justice a reality in an imperfect and human world; about a soul who understands the right thing but can't bring himself to do it; about how it could be that a person could write words that he knows condemn his own activities; about Jefferson "trembling" when he compares his desires with God's justice. Note that calling Jefferson a racist or saying, conversely, that he was simply a man of his times *both* put a barrier between him and us; we don't then know how to talk to him, to ask him questions, or see if there are any *reasons* behind his actions and life. We have made him "other," we have made history "past," and we have learned very little.*

While I can never have Jefferson's biography—I cannot live in his time, I cannot have his friends or his loves, I cannot really

---

* If we can resist contextualizing or historicizing Jefferson, we might well run into some other questions, serious and important questions, that many students will want to understand. Is it *true* that all men are created equal? After all, Jefferson says this idea is not only true but "self-evidently" true. What might that mean? Since Jefferson didn't write that all men were created "the same" but "equal," what did he have in mind? In what way is it possible to say that all men are "equal" when it's obvious that, in so many external ways, we are short and tall, strong and weak, and so on? Moreover, Jefferson mentions equality first, then rights: Do our rights stem from our equality? How so? And what might God and "nature" have to do with this? Further, if we want to say that all "white" men have inalienable rights, how did *they* get them and not other people? Perhaps we can deduce our rights from our common humanity, but how can you draw rights out of "whiteness"? Or out of "maleness"? Since these latter positions seem so clearly nonsensical, do we really want to believe that Jefferson thought they were "self-evident"? These and a hundred other questions—serious questions, questions a people might fight a war and die over—are only possible if we try to understand Jefferson and not dismiss him or excuse him.

sense his pains or feel his emotions—nevertheless, amazingly, I can possess his mind! His times are gone and his body has rotted. Yet, most strangely of all, while I cannot have anything physical or material of his, I can today make what was immaterial in him real. Through the medium of words on a piece of paper or through a book, I can have Jefferson's *ideas*; I can work to make his thoughts my thoughts. How strange it is that the thing that often most lives on after us are our thoughts! *This is the great promise of liberal education—that thoughts and ideas and insights, far from being bound to this time or that place, can transcend time and place and can go from the dead to living teachers and their students.* This is also why historicism, which so closely binds ideas to their time and place, is the enemy of liberal education.

But I wrote above that I also had a positive observation about what I see happening in some good schools. This has to do with the movement away from constant reliance on textbooks and more reliance on original sources. Rather than read *about* the formation of the federal government, why not read some of the debates in the Philadelphia convention, some of *The Federalist Papers*, and a few of the writings of the Anti-Federalists? Rather than read *about* the fall of the Roman republic, perhaps turn to Plutarch and read something from the lives of Cato, Cicero, Caesar, and Antony. Rather than memorize "the five causes of the Civil War" in a secondary text, why not read some Webster, Haynes, Calhoun, and Lincoln? And, after reading them, *why not talk about it in class*? Will your students come to know everything scholars on these subjects know? No. Will they have the benefit of the latest cutting-edge interpretation, supposedly putting to rest the errors of all previous investigators? No. But will they learn to grapple directly with ideas, learn to follow an argument and see the force of its alternative, and learn to read and analyze and start to understand? Yes. And that's enough to start.

"Talk about it in class." The movement away from textbooks is also a movement toward *active* learning. Those of us who teach know that we learned more by teaching than by listening, more than by "absorbing" and repeating. Well, the same is true of our students. The more you can diminish the use of the lecture and the textbook—not eliminate necessarily, but diminish—and the more you can make students active learners and themselves active teachers of their classmates in discussion, the more your students will learn and make learning their own.

Now, as with most general rules, there are exceptions. "What," you might ask, "is to keep a seminar on, say, American history from degenerating into a bull session? What keeps this so-called active learning from becoming just chatter, or the self-indulgent tossing out of feelings, unfounded opinions, and general blah-blah?" Here's where the reading of texts and biographies and speeches comes in. The class should be about what they can draw out of the material, not about their private views on the subject. Bull sessions center on one student's opinions and another's views of the matter. A good seminar focuses on a text, a play, a speech, a biography.

Along these lines, shun all courses such as "*Problems* of American Democracy" or "*Problems* of Religion and Society." Such courses ask to be filled with the random opinions of everyone. Often not much is learned, though students do get to "express themselves." How much better is a course on "Principles of American Democracy" or "The Foundations of Religious Pluralism." At least then students will have to grapple with and discuss ideas other than their own, understand them, and, if the class goes well, learn to compare what they've discovered with their own feelings and sentiments. We go to school to become smarter about things that matter; not to discover that we have our own opinions on this and that or, worse, that everyone should listen.

A Message to High School Seniors

Next year, for the first time in your life, almost everything will depend on you—you, your choices, and the decisions you make. Some of the mistakes you'll make are fixable; some are not. Now I know that I will probably have as much luck as your uncle in shaping your future or helping you make at least mostly fixable mistakes. But I can't help myself, so humor me.

First, of course you're worried about your future. Not to be concerned is irrational. But, please, don't think that what you're interested in today will still hold your interest down the line or that the world will reward you financially twenty years from now because of your current great interest in film or cars or sports.

Still, if you do have a particular interest, see if you can generalize it. Your particular interest in mechanical things might really grow into an interest more generally in engineering. An interest in nature might expand into an interest in biology or astronomy. I've even known people with an interest in cooking to find that they really had an interest in chemistry or in health and then in medicine. At every turn, try to generalize, try to broaden your particular interests. Check out where your interests might lead, not where they end.

230 | THE DEATH OF LEARNING

Second, if you have an interest in the liberal arts or in some aspects of them, have enough strength to stick to it. I know, there will be voices telling you to do something more immediately "practical," something that, today, will set you up for life. *For life*—do you know how scary a thought that is, especially if you're narrowing yourself down simply because you think you need to get yourself into the workforce? No, it's better to have some courage. If in your soul is the desire to see the world of nature and the works of man, and to see them all in their amazing predictability as well as their frightening complexity, then hold to that desire. The liberal arts open no particular vocational door for you, but neither do they close very many. Do not make your world too small too fast.

Third, the opposite of a narrow education may well be a "broad" education, but it is never a "scattered" education. Having your first few years of college—or even all of college—introduce you to your civilization and its works, show you important parts of the world that are not your culture, take you into the world of science and mathematics, have you read good literature, study history, learn other languages, and think philosophically about important issues of politics, economics, liberty, and ethics—all this is excellent. But too many colleges think they have a liberal arts program if they give you hundreds of courses to pick from, without helping you pick out the more important from the less, the more basic from the narrow and small. A liberal education isn't a scattered, smorgasbord, incoherent education. It isn't dilettantism. A person who studies philosophy, world history, languages, literature, math, and science is on his or her way to being liberally educated. A person who takes a few courses in deviant psychology, pottery, creative writing, history of sports, and how to be a good consumer isn't.

Fourth, here's an almost invariable rule when looking at colleges: A fat catalogue is no indication of a good education. Indeed, a university that has thousands of offerings and tosses them all at you saying, "You pick and choose," has no interest in helping you become seriously educated.* A fat catalogue often says more about the research interests of the professors than about their interest in being partners with you in making sense of your education. Indeed, a college with a thin catalogue might actually have a faculty concerned about the intellectual grounding and shape of your mind, not simply about its wandering.

This all leads to a fifth point, one that few students and virtually no parents will accept: When it comes to colleges and universities, most bad reputations are deserved, but many good reputations are not. In fact, most universities with good reputations have it because of their stellar graduate/research faculty, not because of the excellence of their undergraduate teaching. If you're going to graduate school, go to the most highly rated one you can get into. If you're looking for an undergraduate liberal arts education, look at the program of studies they each offer; look at the dedication of the faculty to undergraduate teaching; look a bit at class size; and look to see that the college and its faculty have an interest, as I put it before, in partnering with you in the pursuit of your education.

A corollary of this is that a "university" is not ipso facto better than a "college." I know that there are many colleges that have become "universities" simply because that word carries, they think, greater cachet. Sorry I have to tell you—*it ain't so.* I've attended both colleges and universities in my life; I've taught at some excellent colleges and some fine universities. And, aside from the inferiority complex some professors get from hearing

---

* Recently, the Harvard catalogue ran to 860 pages. That was surely a great help.

all the time that universities are really "better" and that colleges are just baby universities, I will tell you honestly that some of the finest teaching and learning takes place in colleges and not in universities. I know, it feeds your ego to say you go to an Ivy League university or one of the major state universities. But don't think you're getting a better education than at a small, residential, liberal arts college; I honestly doubt it.

Sixth: Everyone hopes that when you go to college you'll get straight As. Well, I don't. Now, with grade inflation being what it is, not getting all As may mean that you're not all that bright, which is possible; or that you frittered away your time playing and partying, which is probable; or that you avoided easy courses and took at least a few hard subjects, subjects that were new to you but that were important, informative, and interesting. All As might mean you're a polymath genius. It more likely means you took easy courses, never challenged yourself, and never found a professor who pushed you to the limit. Try to remember: few people are good at physics and literature and philosophy all together. But an educated person knows something, perhaps a lot, about all three—therefore, an educated person rarely gets all As. An educated person gets decent grades in great courses, not great grades in merely decent courses.

All this is not something to get you off the hook with your parents because you've been partying instead of studying. Nor is it, I hope, a cheap rationalization for all my own less-than-perfect report cards. But I can tell you that, as time goes on, no one will ever ask you why you only got a B and not an A in Medieval History. Or, if they do, tell them it was an amazing course taught by a great professor in which your mind became open to important things you hardly imagined before and you wouldn't trade it for all the easy As in all those easy courses ever.

Acknowledgments

First, I need to thank my wife, Catherine, without whose friendship and help for over fifty years this book would not have been possible. So long as we could have coffee together in the morning, cocktails at 5:00, and dinner by 7:00, I could spend months and years with scraps of notes working quietly—or frantically—typing away. Cathy, thank you.

There are those who gave me actual, material help in the writing of this book: President Andrew T. Ford of Wabash College, who asked me to be the first research fellow at the Lilly Center for the Study of the Liberal Arts; Robert George and Brad Wilson of the James Madison Program at Princeton; Carole Iannone and Steve Balch of the National Association of Scholars, whose journal, *Academic Questions*, published so many of my higher education musings; my editor Felicia Chernesky; the dedicated team at Encounter—Amanda DeMatto and Mary Spencer; copyeditor Barbie Halaby; and all those who read parts of the manuscript and with help or criticism helped me frame the argument: Michael Poliakoff, Joshua Mitchell, George Ball, Karl Haigler, David Bolotin, and many others.

Then there are those whose writings or whose conversations with me over the years had an impact on my thinking—Eva Brann, Douglas Preston, Warren Winiarski, Bill McClay, Eric Brown, John Leo, Leon Kass, John Shelton Reed, and Werner Gundersheimer. Sadly, some of those who had the deepest influence on my thinking, like Werner Dannhauser and Allan Bloom, are now gone.

Finally, I want to thank the first students at the American University of Iraq in Sulaimani, which I helped start and where I taught and served. Yes, many if not most of them, because of interest or necessity, went beyond the liberal arts and succeeded in other important areas. But the excitement, the wonder, that filled their eyes and minds when they were first introduced to civilization's greatest writers, thinkers, and ideas was, to me, astonishing. It proved James Madison correct in this as in so many other things: that nothing is more edifying in a nation than liberty and learning, each leaning on the other for their mutual and surest support.

Index

Page numbers followed by n indicate notes.

Latin language. *See* ancient languages
learning about and learning from, 21, 113–20, 219
Lewis, C. S., 113–14, 115
"liberal," proper understanding of word, 16–17
Liberal Arts at the Brink (Ferrall), 28, 53
liberal arts education, generally, x, 13–14; academic subjects common to, 16, 16n, 19–20; attacked from within and "suicide" of, 6, 29, 86–91; as both radical and conservative, 22, 139–40; conserving function of, 160–61; and consideration of issues of human life, 20–21, 55, 57–58, 59, 131–33, 132n; decline in status of, 25–29, 37–38, 48–49, 83–91; flawed teaching of, 4–6, 113–14; Founders and value of, 31–35, 41–42; as freeing individuals to think for themselves, 17–20, 21; learning about and learning from, 113–20; learning about one's own culture and, 135–38, 137n; learning "for its own sake" and, 15, 15n; "politics" and, 14, 154–55; specialization and narrowing of disciplines, 57–64, 59n; tasks and goals of, 139–40, 139n, 146, 149–50; value to future and magic of learning from past, 121–25
"Liberal Scholarship and the College Teacher" (Simpson), 62n
Lincoln, Abraham, 123, 145; classical and historical knowledge of, 34–35, 150–51, 156–57, 175–86; historical context and reading of, 217; slavery and, 180–82, 205
literature: learning about and learning from, 113–20, 219; in liberal arts education, 19–20; Lincoln's self-education and, 176–79; literary criticism and, 143. *See also* reading, politics of
Luther, Martin, 216

Macbeth (Shakespeare), 177–78
Madison, James, 35, 123, 145, 157, 159, 159n, 174, 184, 234
Middle East, specialization of education and, 59–60. *See also* American University of Iraq in Sulaimani (AUIS)
MIT Lecture Series, 199–200
moderation, cultivated by education, 154–55, 199–200
moral relativism, 155n
multiculturalism and diversity movements: aims of, 73–74; characteristics of serious,

honest multicultural curricula, 71–73; core curricula and, 88–89; evolution to separation and narrow worldviews, 70–71; Kors, Silverglate, and higher education, 193–201; as lacking qualities of self-criticism, 90; liberal arts education and, 43, 48; politicization of Western civilization curriculum and, 65–66; rejection of common culture, 58, 71, 80; Stanford's dismantling of Western civilization curricula, x–xi, 67–70, 84, 88, 182–89, 187n, 188n, 199; stigmatization of the ordinary and, 102–3

naïve questions, value of asking, 118–19, 145–47
Newman, John Henry, 151–53, 159–60, 161
non-liberal education. *See* vocational and professional education
North Dakota State University, 98n

Oberlin College, 89n, 90n
ordinariness, liberal education and, 151
ordinary values, stigmatizing of, 93–107, 139; cultural transformation and, 98, 102–4; indoctrination and, 96, 96–97n, 102–4, 105–6; political correctness and, 94–95, 100–102, 101n; pushback to, 98–100

Paine, Thomas, 85
parents, usefulness of liberal arts education and, 38–39, 141
Penrod and Sam (Tarkington), 2–3, 7, 135
personal and societal goods: education and, 111–13; individual benefits of liberal education, 149–55, 161; societal benefits of liberal education, 156–61
Pettit, John, 204n
philosophy: in liberal arts education, 19; Lincoln's self-education and, 179–82
Plato, 59n
poets, 141, 141n
political correctness and speech codes, 8, 76, 76n, 84, 94–95, 98, 100–102, 101n, 106, 190, 193–201
politics: curricular changes and indoctrination, not education, 75–81, 79n; liberal arts education generally and, 14, 154–55. *See also* reading, politics of
Princeton University, 99
private good. *See* personal and societal goods
Ps, 128, 141, 141n